Playford for Mandolin

121 Tunes from the

Playford Dancing Masters (1651-1728)

adapted for Mandolin

by John Goodin

WWW.MELBAY.COM

Introduction

In 1651 John Playford published a small book titled *The English Dancing Master or Plaine and easie Rules for the Dancing of Country Dances, with the Tune to each Dance.* A second edition was published the next year, without the word English in the title, and new editions continued to appear until around 1728. New editions generally added some new tunes and dances and dropped some of the old ones.

The tunes contained in these volumes appear as single melody lines followed by dance instructions. For this book I have chosen 121 of these melodies and present them in both standard notation and mandolin tablature, along with chord symbols. In addition I have changed the keys of many tunes to render them more mandolin-friendly. My main source has been the 1985 collection edited by Jeremy Barlow titled *The Complete Country Dance Tunes from Playford's Dancing Master (1651-ca.1728)* which contains 535 distinct tunes in modern standard notation, many with optional variations. I also consulted several other modern collections that contain Playford tunes, most notably the two volumes of English country dance tunes published by Peter Barnes.

Many of the tunes in this book have been played by musicians for their own enjoyment and for dancing for over 300 years. They have endured many changes in fashion and style and today offer us the opportunity to both respect our musical forebears and to forge our own interpretations of these now ancient melodies.

One practical suggestion is to resist the urge to treat these tunes as modern jigs and reels. Try playing them slowly, try them at different tempos. While there may be a more or less historically correct tempo for certain kinds of dance, the melodies themselves can all be treated as listening pieces. Don't feel bound by my suggested chords. These tunes can be harmonized in many ways and they all sound fine without any harmony at all. Likewise feel free to try them in different keys. Playford tunes are resilient and flexible. I hope you enjoy your time with them.

About the Author

John Goodin (1951-) is from southern Indiana and began playing the guitar shortly after seeing the Beatles on *The Ed Sullivan Show* in February of 1964. Ten years later he began to play the mandolin. He has played in many bands and ensembles performing music in a variety of styles and was a founding member of the Louisville Mandolin Orchestra in 1988. Along with studying folk, jazz and pop music he has attended workshops offered by many of today's finest classical mandolinists and he is a long-time member of the Classical Mandolin Society of America.

As a composer Goodin has written dozens of pieces for mandolin orchestra that have been performed and recorded by mandolin orchestras in Europe, Australia, Japan and the United States. Joachim-Trekel-Musikverlag has published four of these mandolin orchestra pieces, *The Louisville Suite* (1995), *Heavens On Earth* (2006), *Antonina* (2015) and *The North Georgia Hills* (2016). His contra dance band, Contratopia, has recorded over 40 of his tunes on their four CDs: *Hands Four, Ballroom Echoes, Smitten* and *Riff City.* Additionally, he has released a duo CD with fiddler Erik Sessions, *Notes from the Farm* (2012), and two solo CDs, *Mandolin Tunes* (2011) and *Deer Tracks for Solo Mandolin* (2013).

Mel Bay Publications published Goodin's book *Telemann for Mandolin* in 2010 and his edition of *12 Divertimentos for Solo Mandolin by James Oswald* in 2016. He has self-published the *Contratopia Tunebook* (with Erik Sessions, 2001), *31 Waltzes* (2009), *Midwestern Mandolin Duos* (2010) and *Postcards From the Crater* (2016). His music has also appeared in Don Julin's *Mandolin for Dummies,* August Watters' book *Exploring Classical Mandolin* and volume 3 of the *Portland Collection.* Goodin has lived in Decorah, Iowa since 1994 where he is now an emeritus associate professor affiliated with Luther College.

Contents

Alchurch

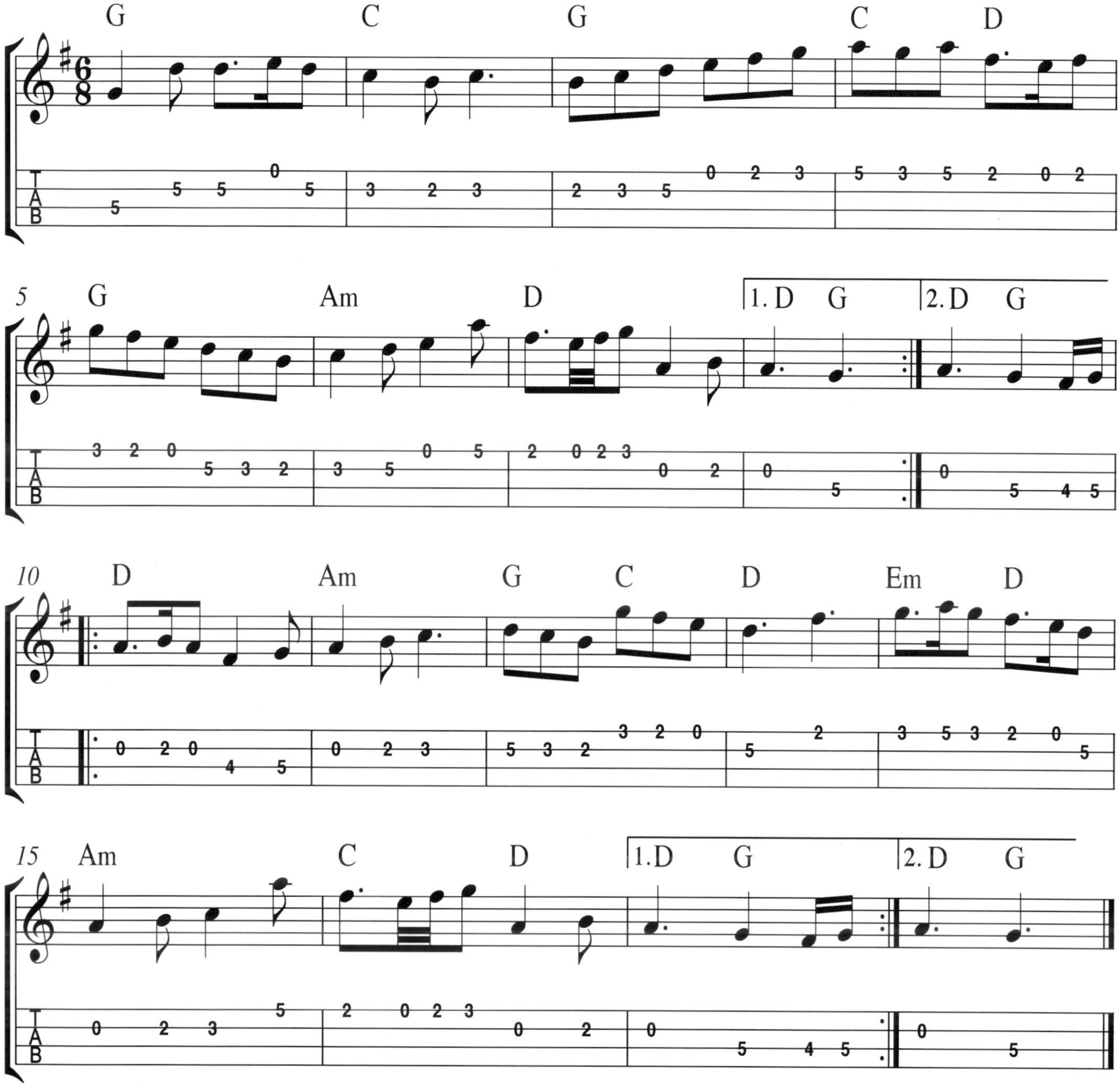
G C G C D
G Am D 1. D G 2. D G
D Am G C D Em D
Am C D 1.D G 2. D G

All in a Garden Green

Amaryllis

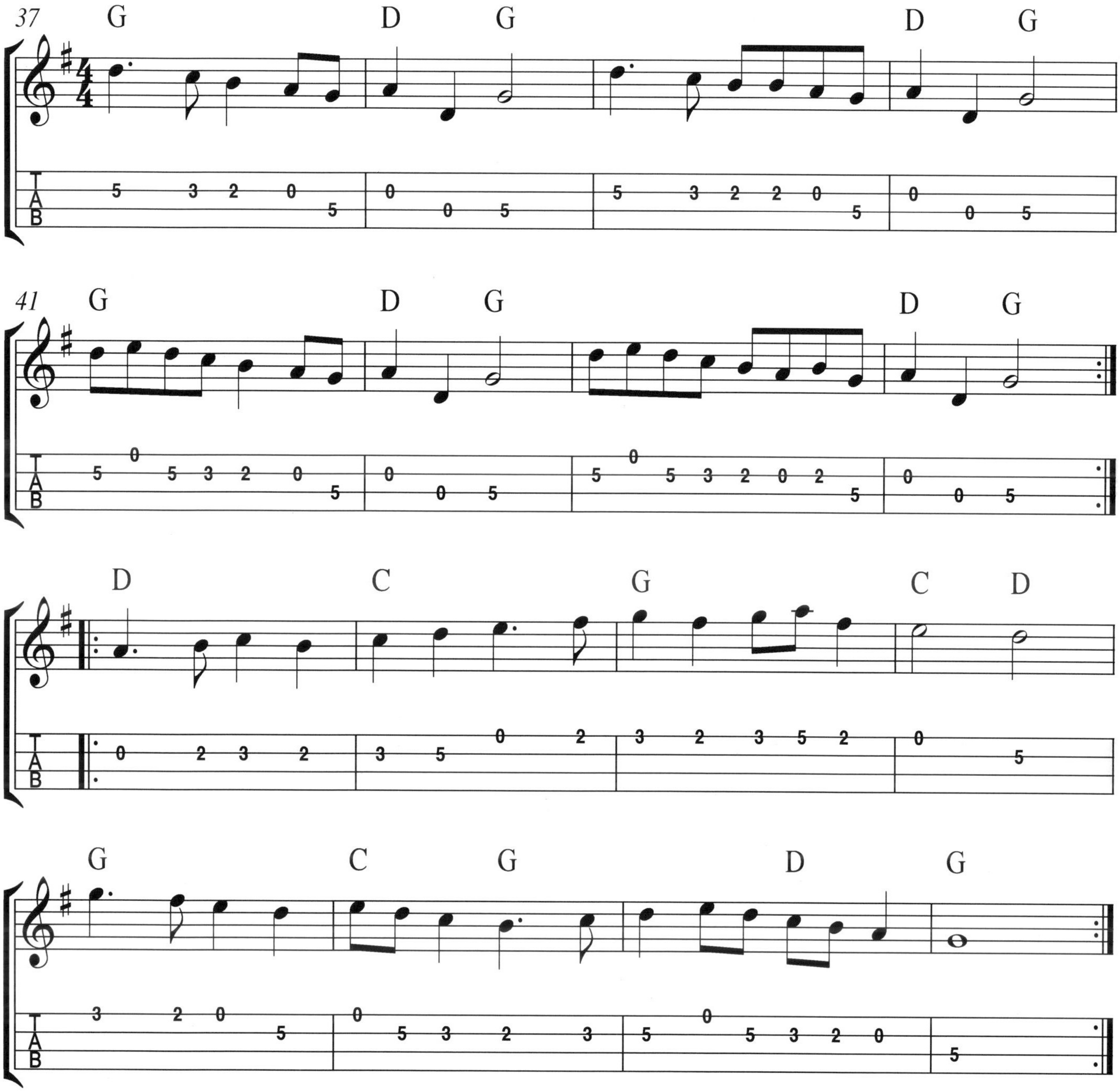
37 G D G D G
41 G D G D G
D C G C D
G C G D G

Apley House

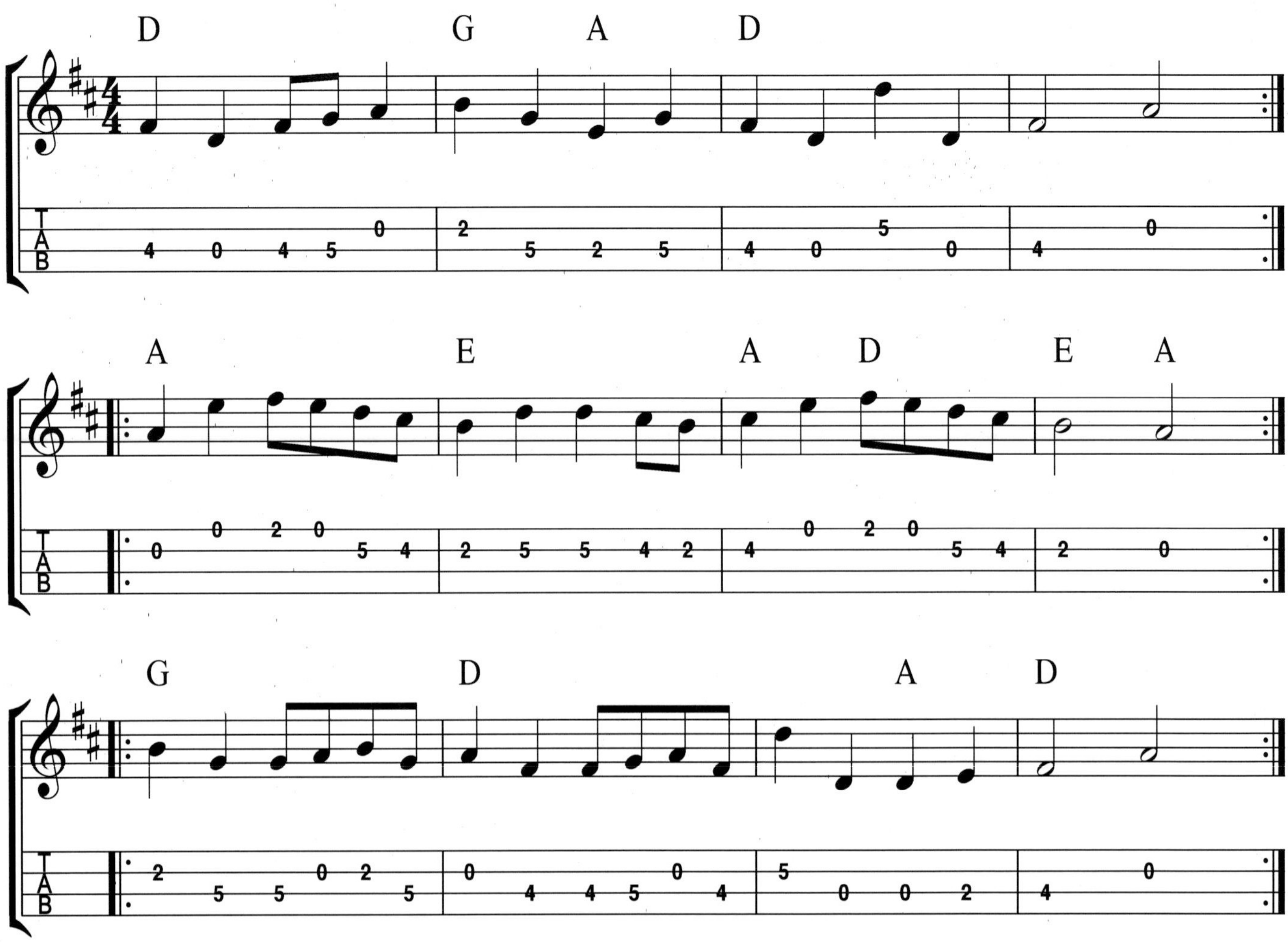
D G A D
A E A D E A
G D A D

Argiers

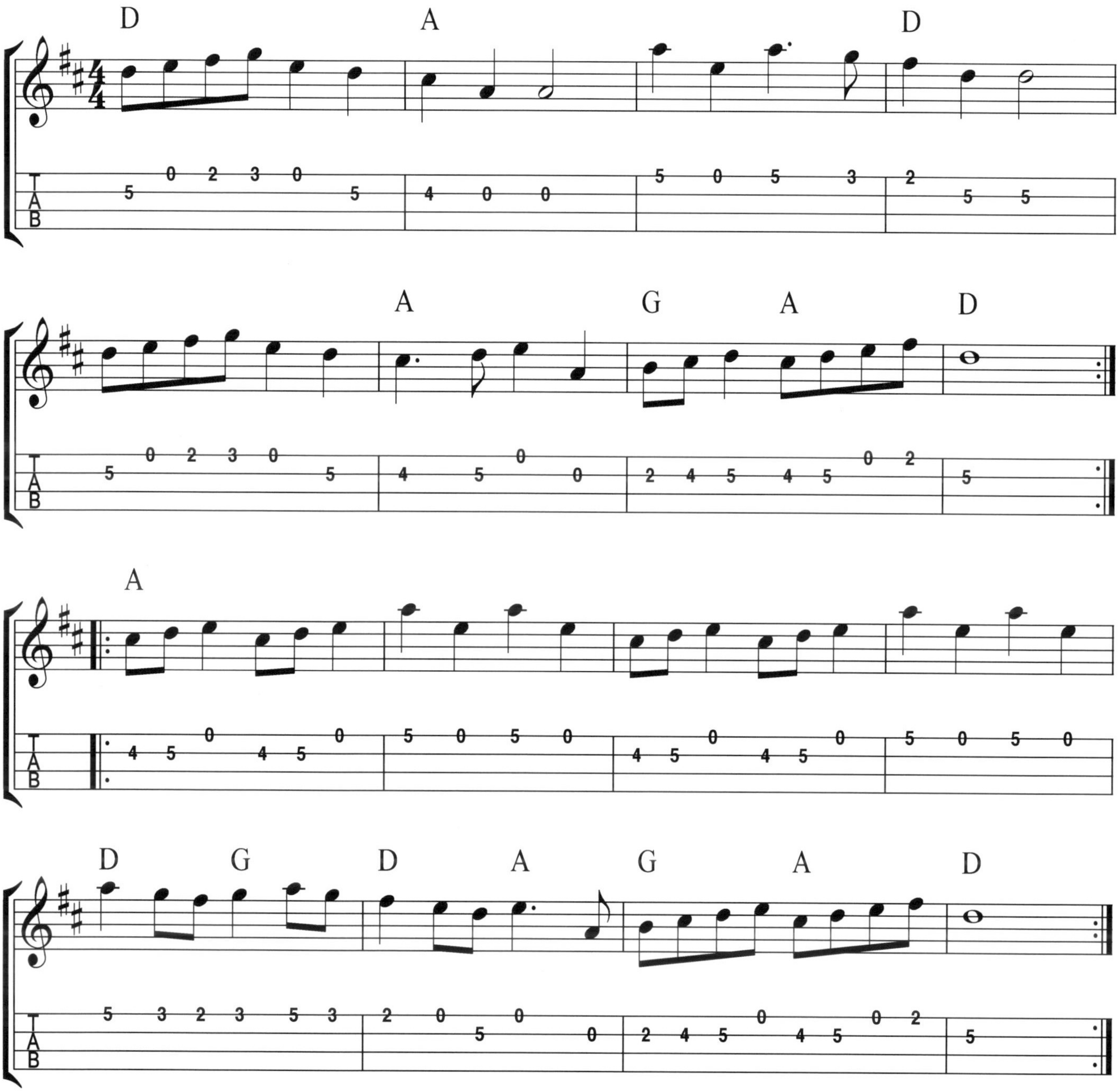
D A D
A G A D
A
D G D A G A D

Bartholomew Fair

Bellamira

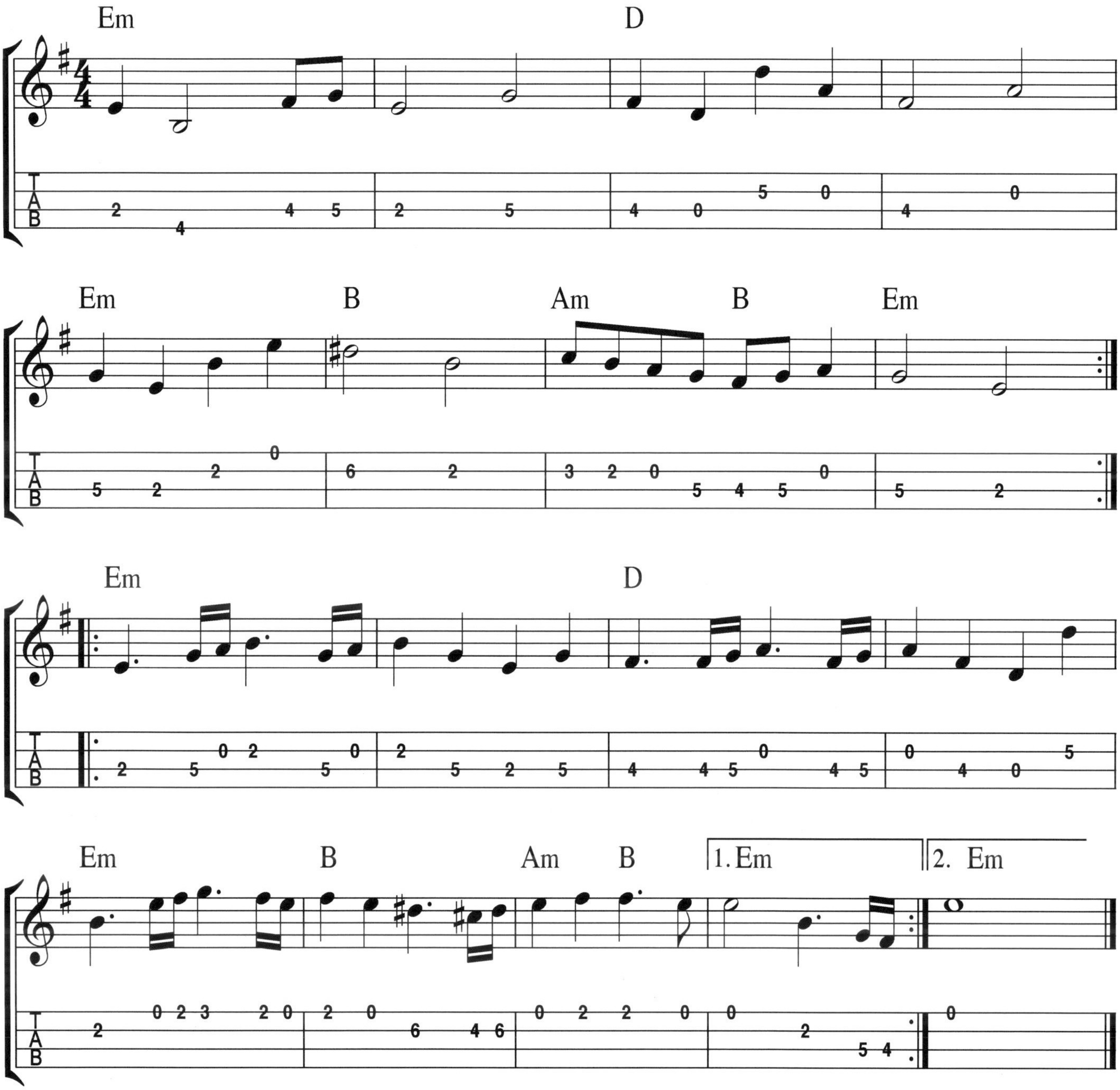
Em
D
Em
B
Am
B
Em
Em
D
Em
B
Am
B
1. Em
2. Em

The Bishop of Bangor's Jig

Black and Grey

Blackheath

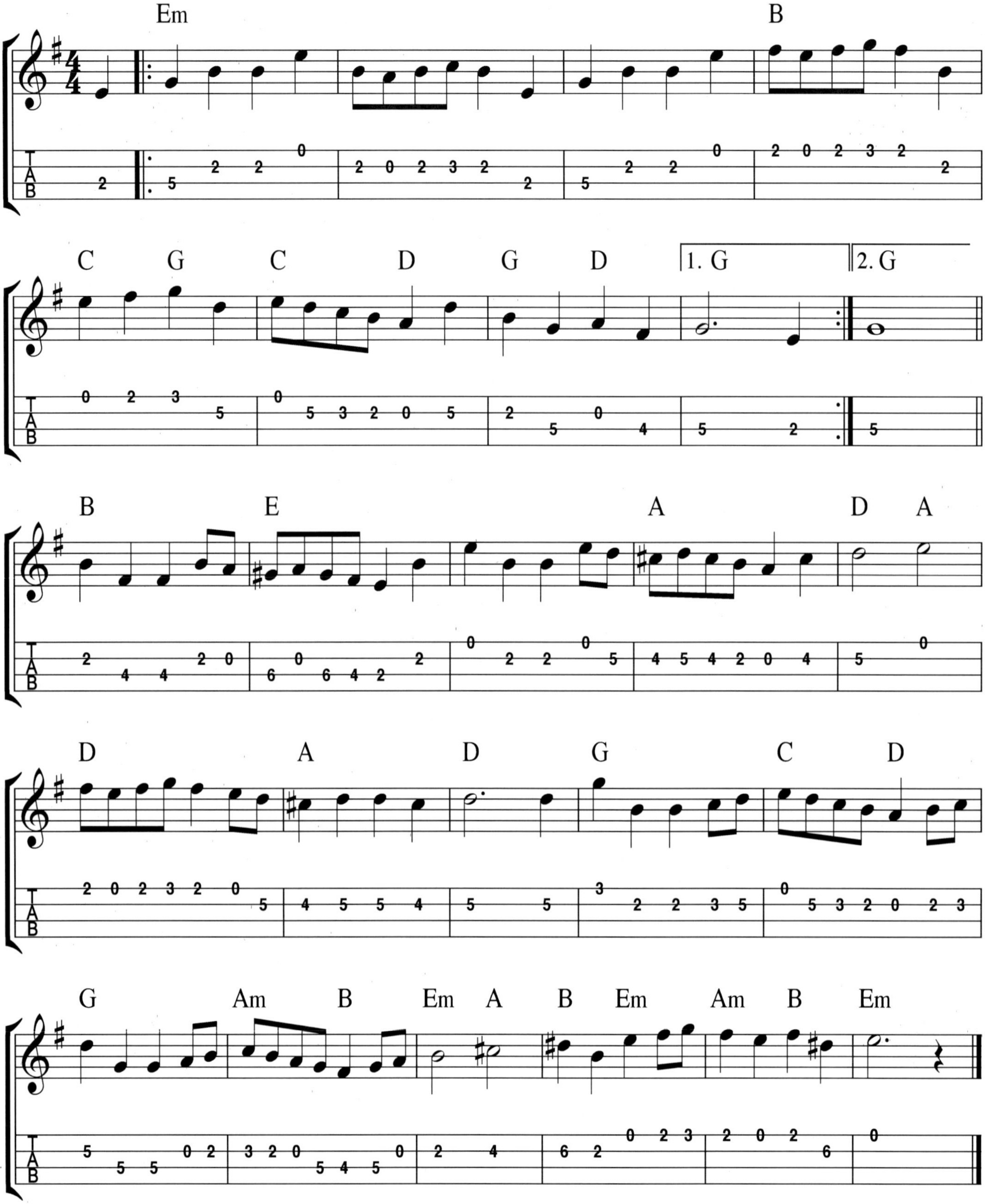
Em B
C G C D G D 1. G 2. G
B E A D A
D A D G C D
G Am B Em A B Em Am B Em

Boatman

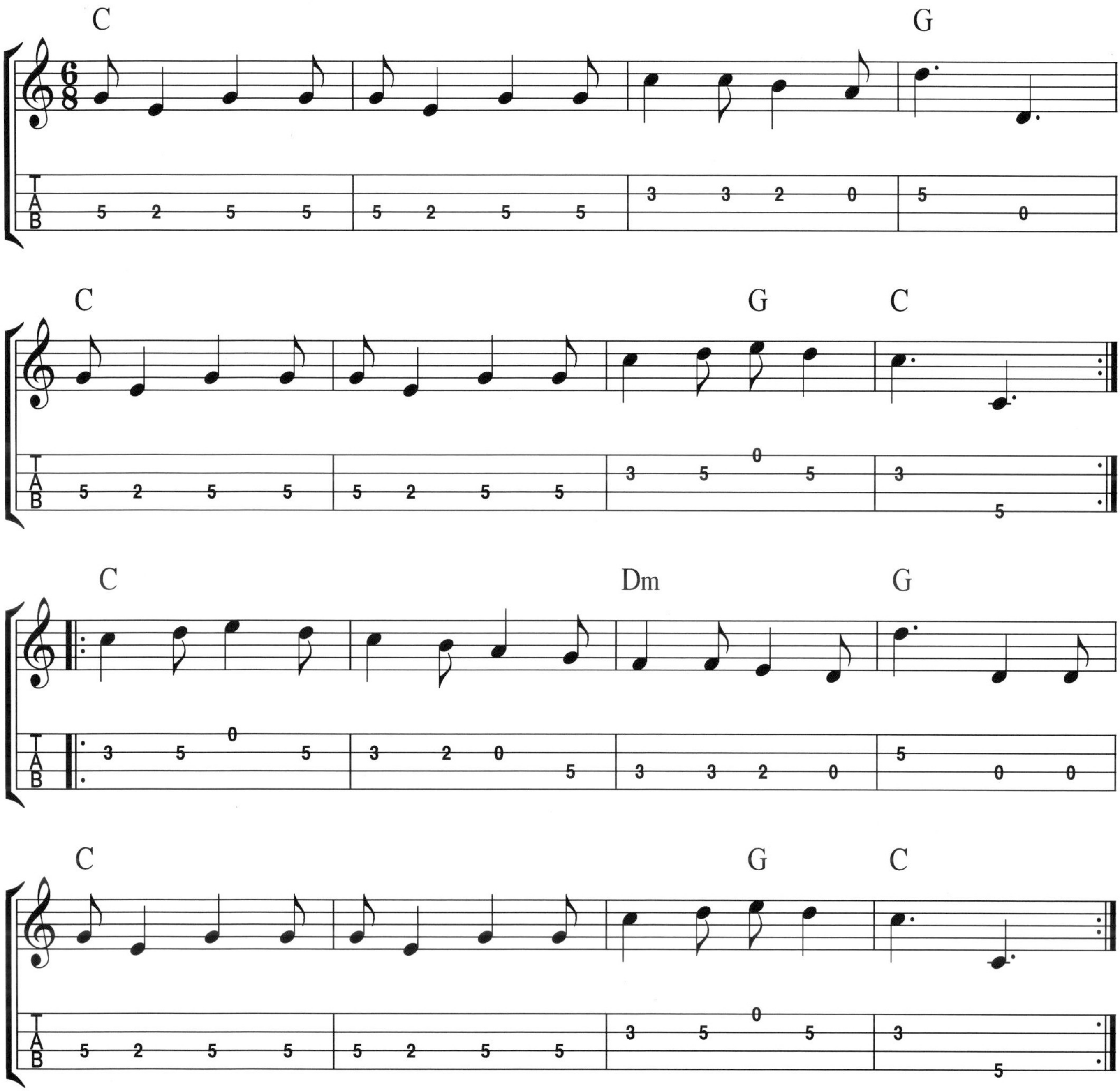
C G
C G C
C Dm G
C G C

Bonny Dundee

Bonny Grey-Ey'd Morn

Bouzer Castle

Bury Fair

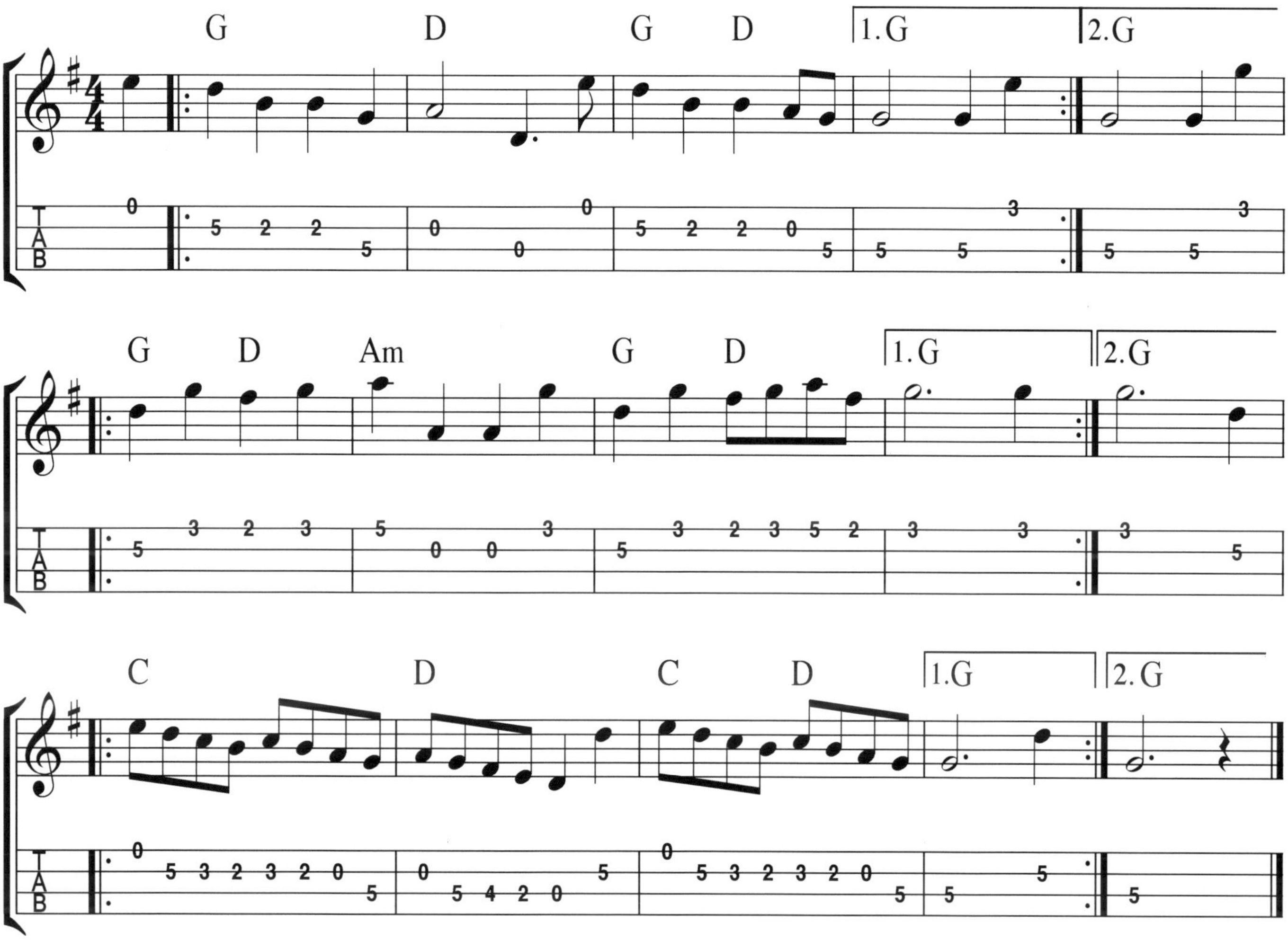
G D G D 1.G 2.G
G D Am G D 1.G 2.G
C D C D 1.G 2.G

Buskin

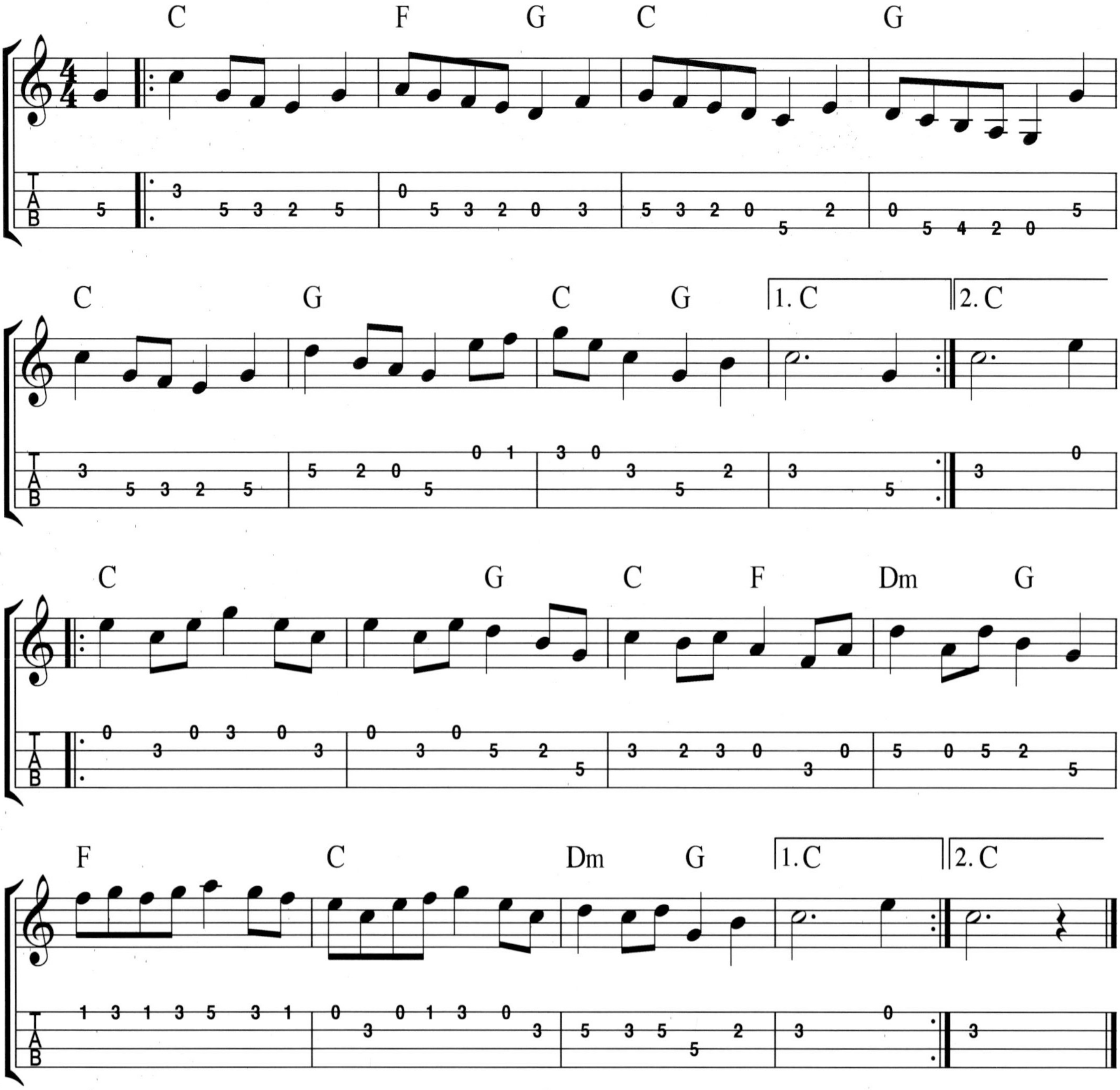
C F G C G
C G C G 1. C 2. C
C G C F Dm G
F C Dm G 1. C 2. C

Captain's Maggot

Chelsea Reach

Cherry Garden

Chestnut

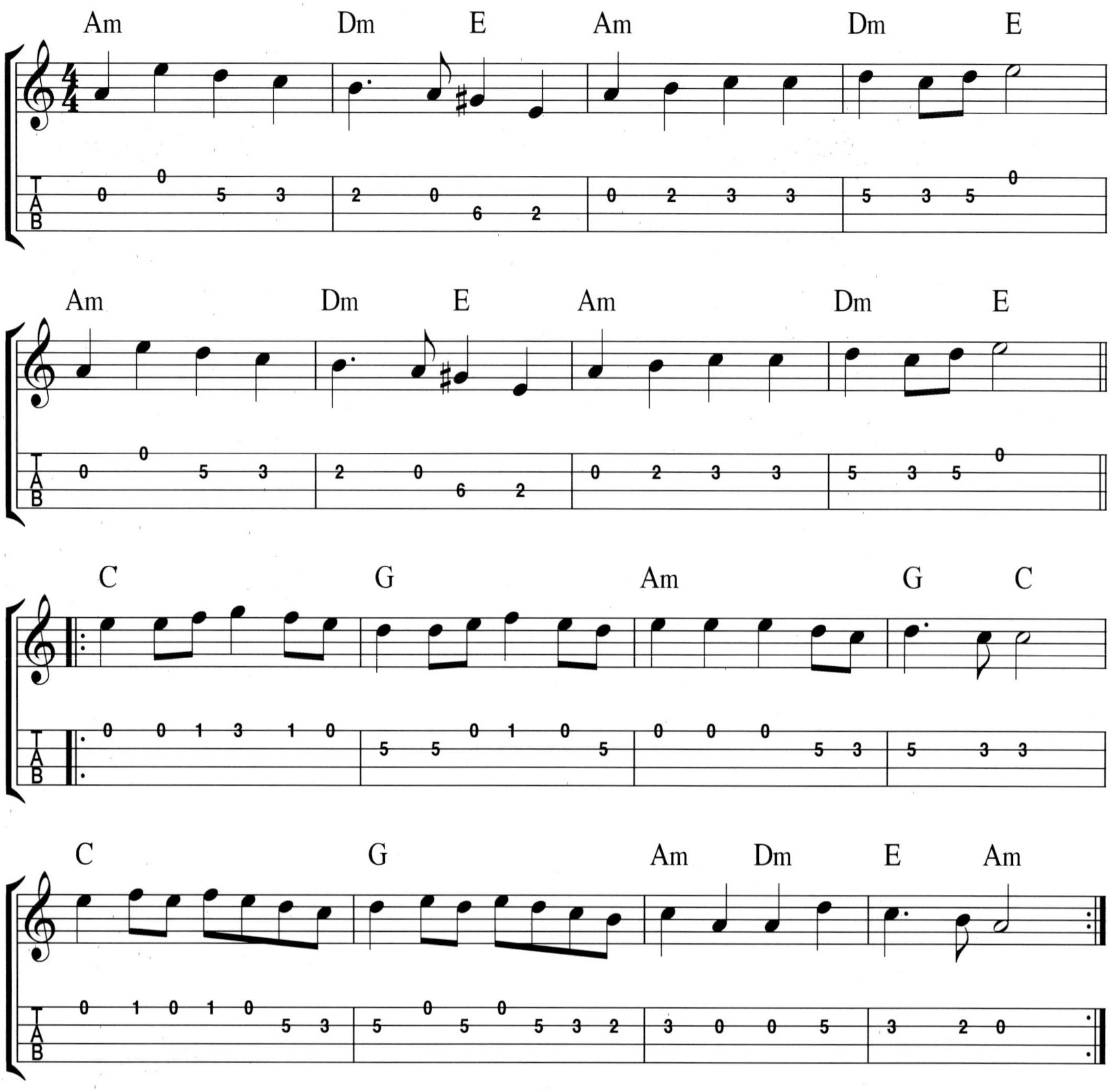
Am Dm E Am Dm E
T
A
B
Am Dm E Am Dm E
C G Am G C
C G Am Dm E Am

Childgrove

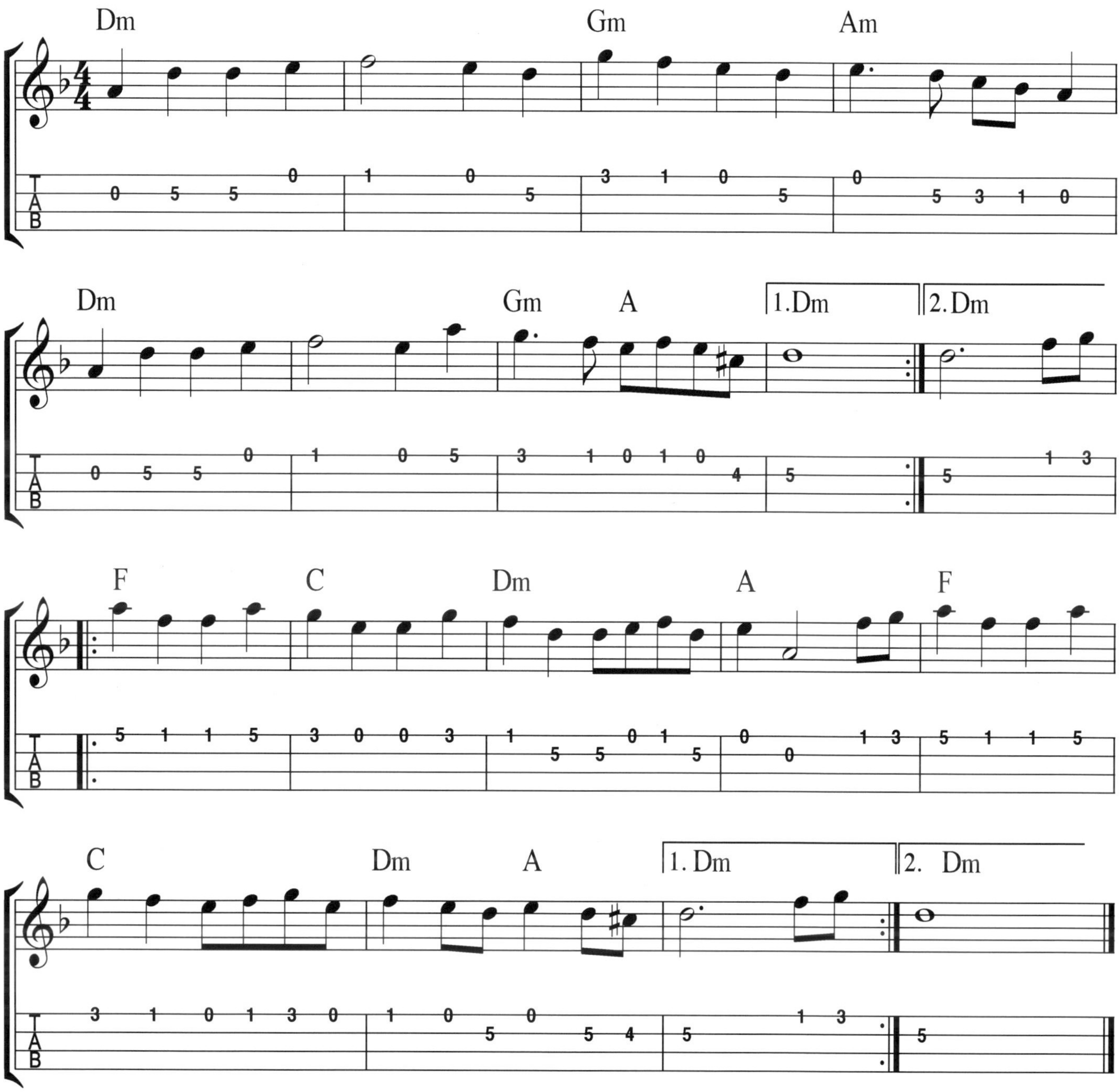
Dm
Gm
Am
Dm
Gm
A
1.Dm
2.Dm
F
C
Dm
A
F
C
Dm
A
1. Dm
2. Dm

Christchurch Bells

Christmas Cheer

Cockleshells

The Coronation Day

Count Tallard

The Country Farmer

Coxes Dance

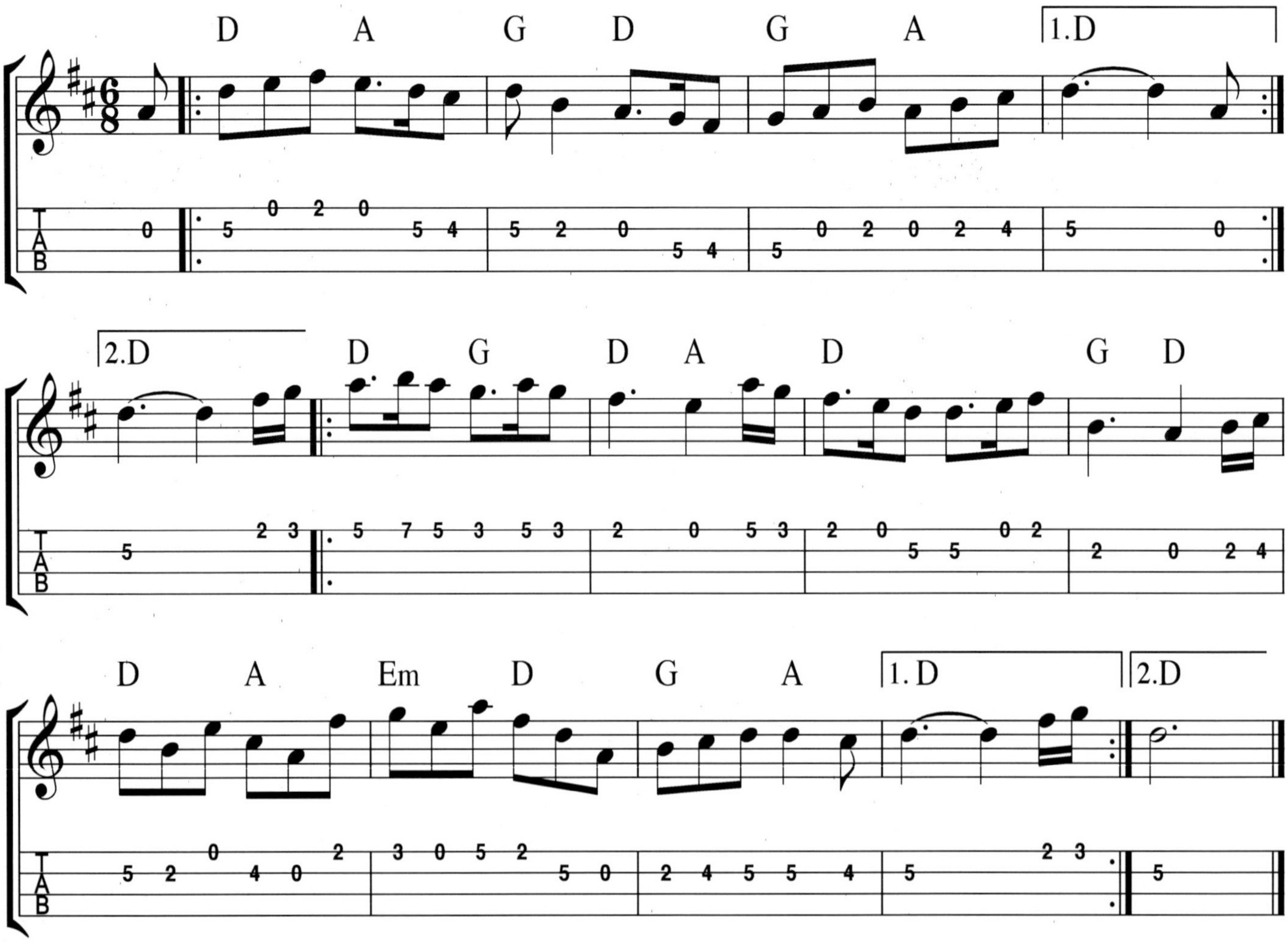
D A G D G A 1.D
2.D D G D A D G D
D A Em D G A 1. D 2.D

Cuckolds All in a Row

Daphne

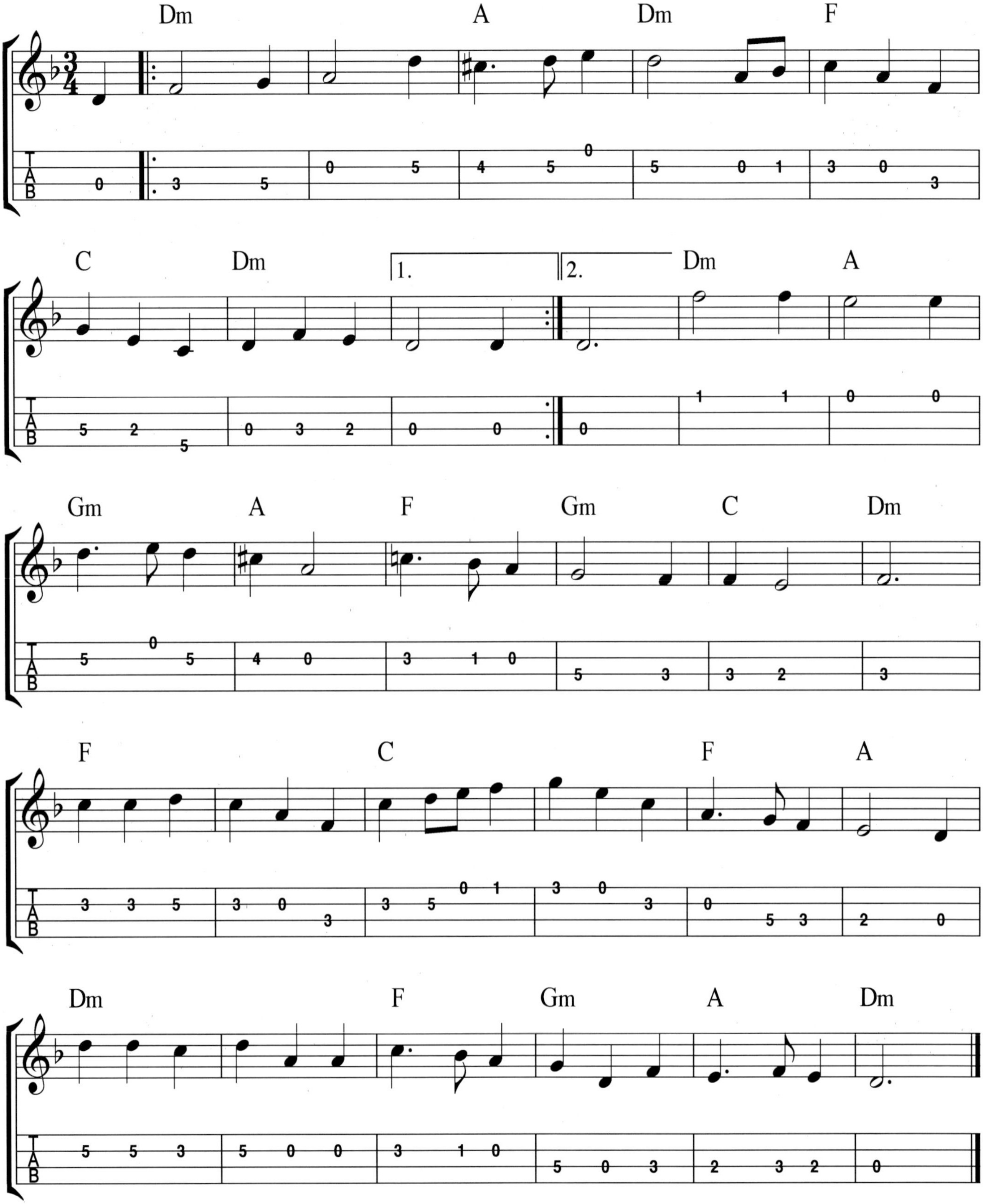
Dm A Dm F
C Dm 1. 2. Dm A
Gm A F Gm C Dm
F C F A
Dm F Gm A Dm

Dragoon's March

Drive the Cold Winter Away

The Duke of Gloucester's March

Duke of Grafton's March

Duke of York's March

Dull Sir John

Easter Eve

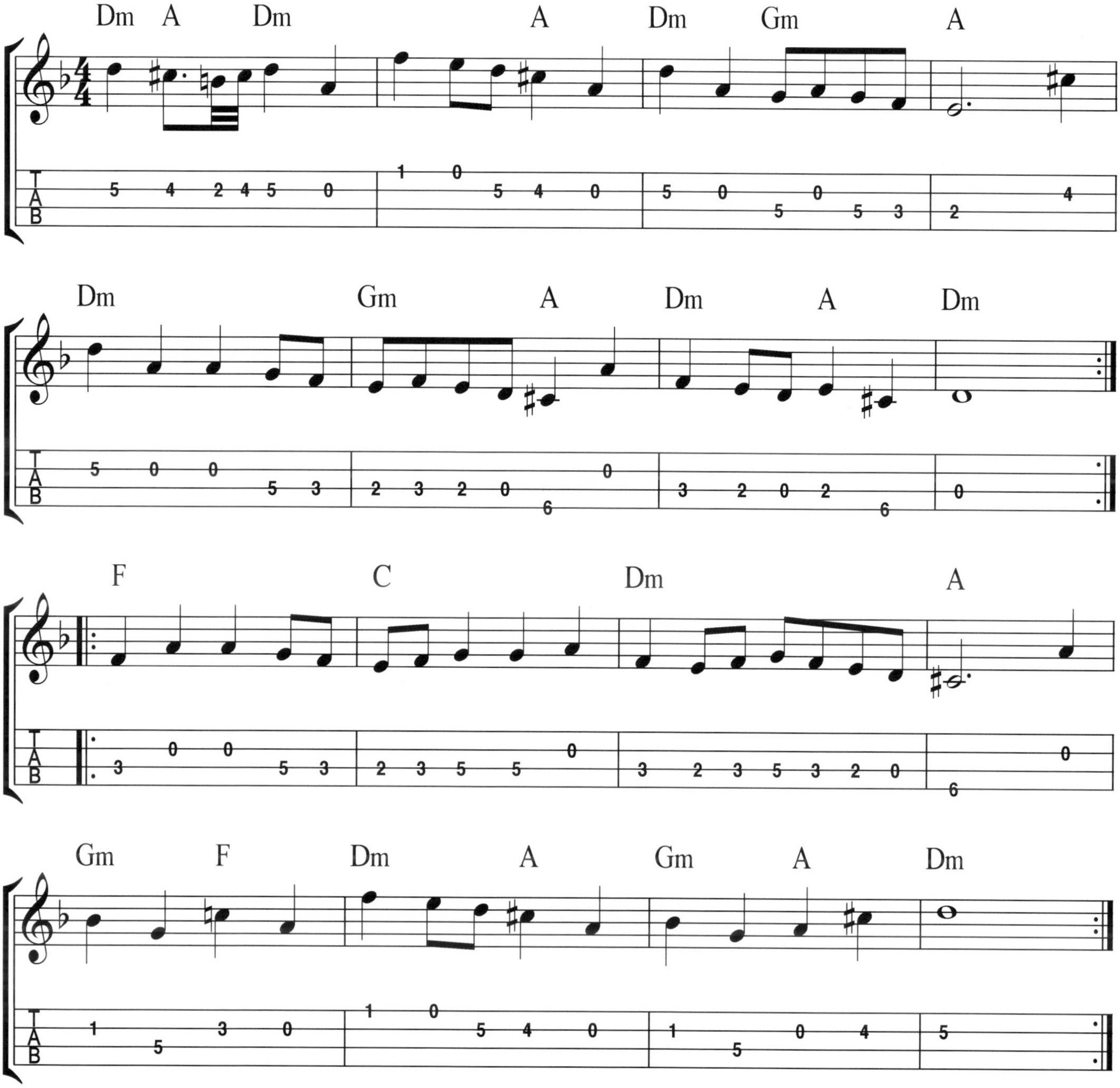
Dm A Dm A Dm Gm A
Dm Gm A Dm A Dm
F C Dm A
Gm F Dm A Gm A Dm

Easter Tuesday

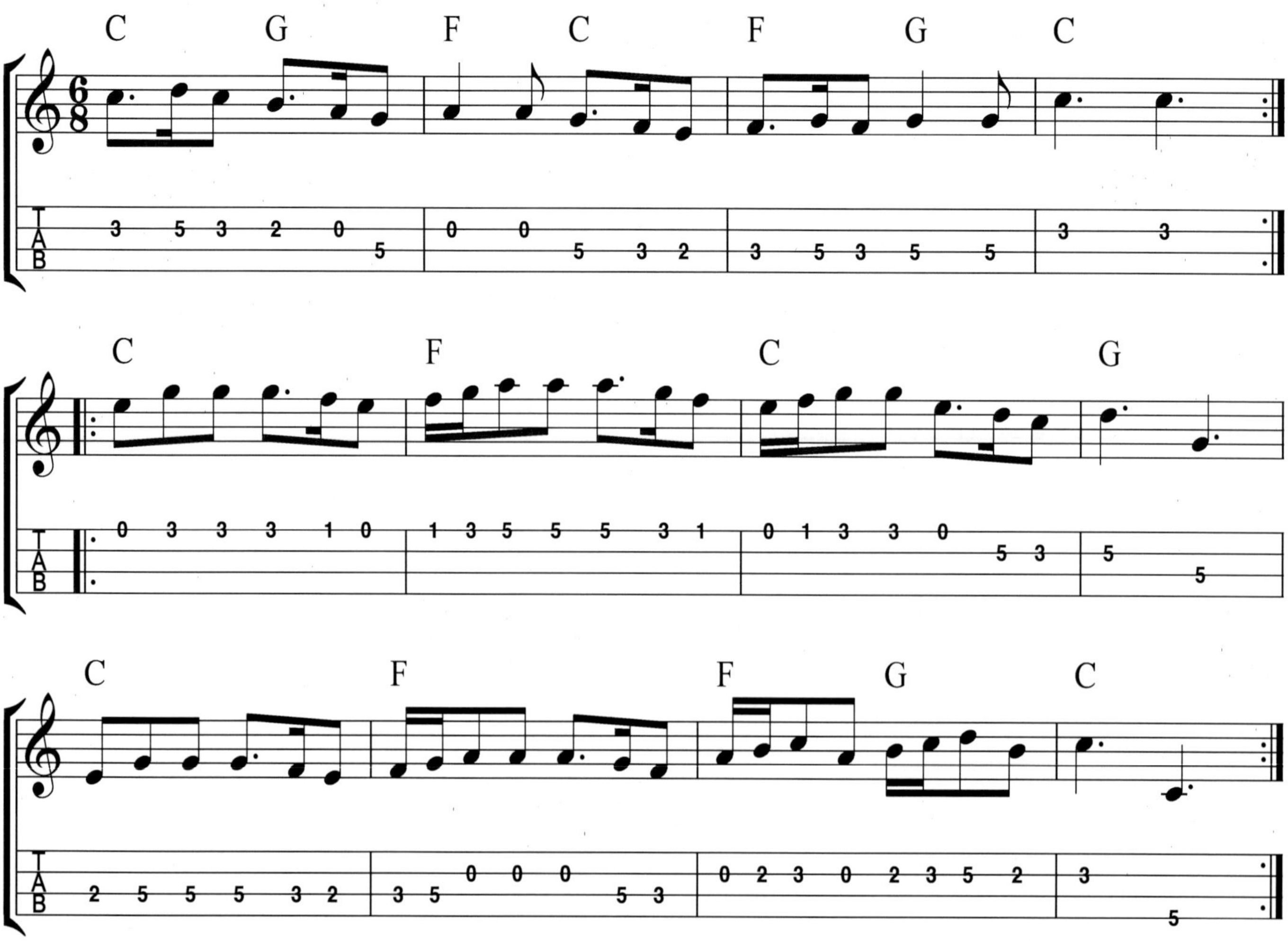

Ely Court

Dm A Dm F C
Dm A Dm Gm A
Dm F C B♭ Dm A
Dm F Gm A Dm C
Dm B♭ A 1. Dm 2. Dm

Epping Forest

A Figure Dance

The Fine Companion

Freeman's Dance

The French Ambassador

The Frolic

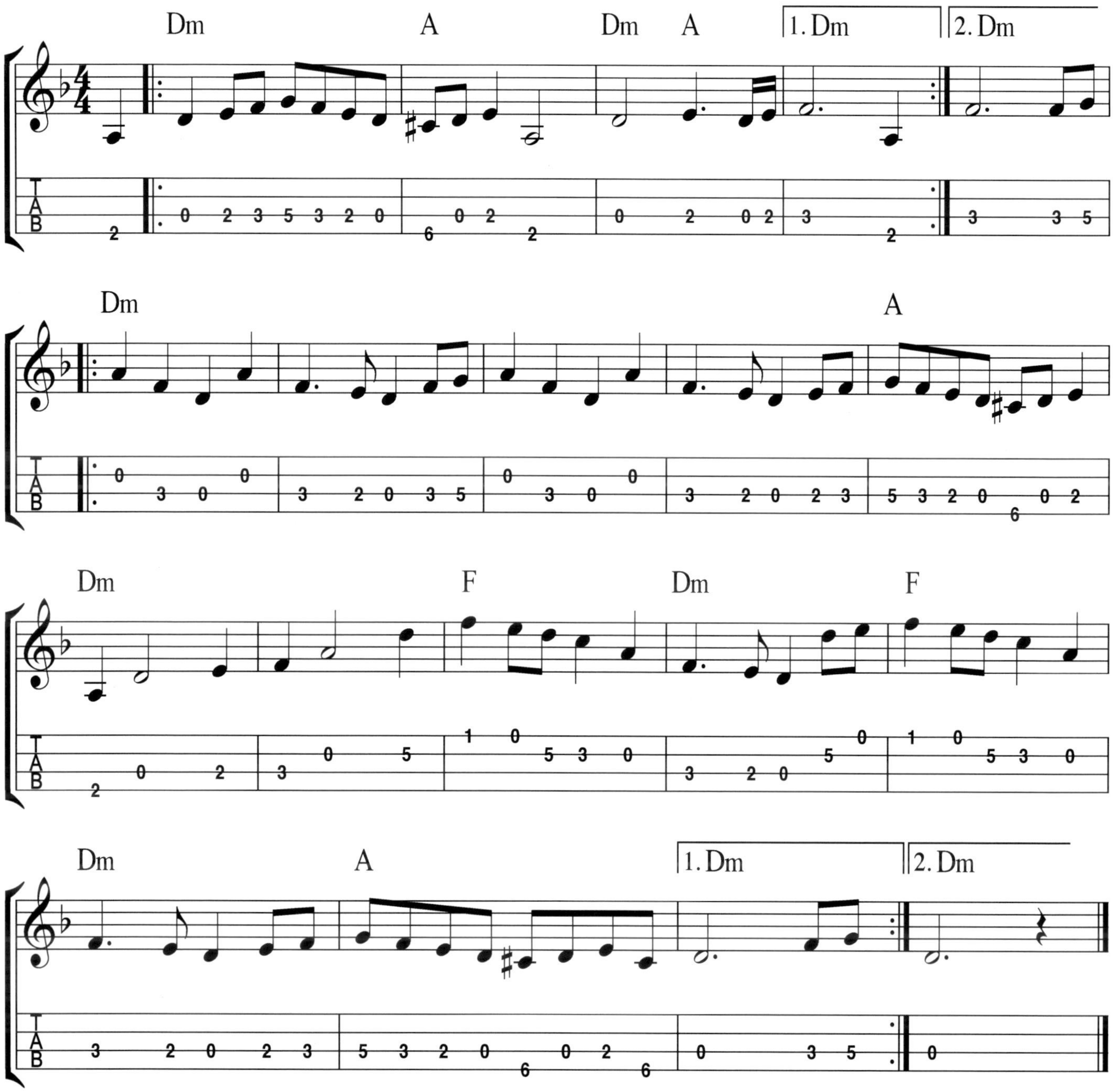
Dm
A
Dm A
1. Dm
2. Dm
Dm
A
Dm
F
Dm
F
Dm
A
1. Dm
2. Dm

From Aberdeen

Fy, Nay, Prithee John

Glory of the Sun

Goddesses

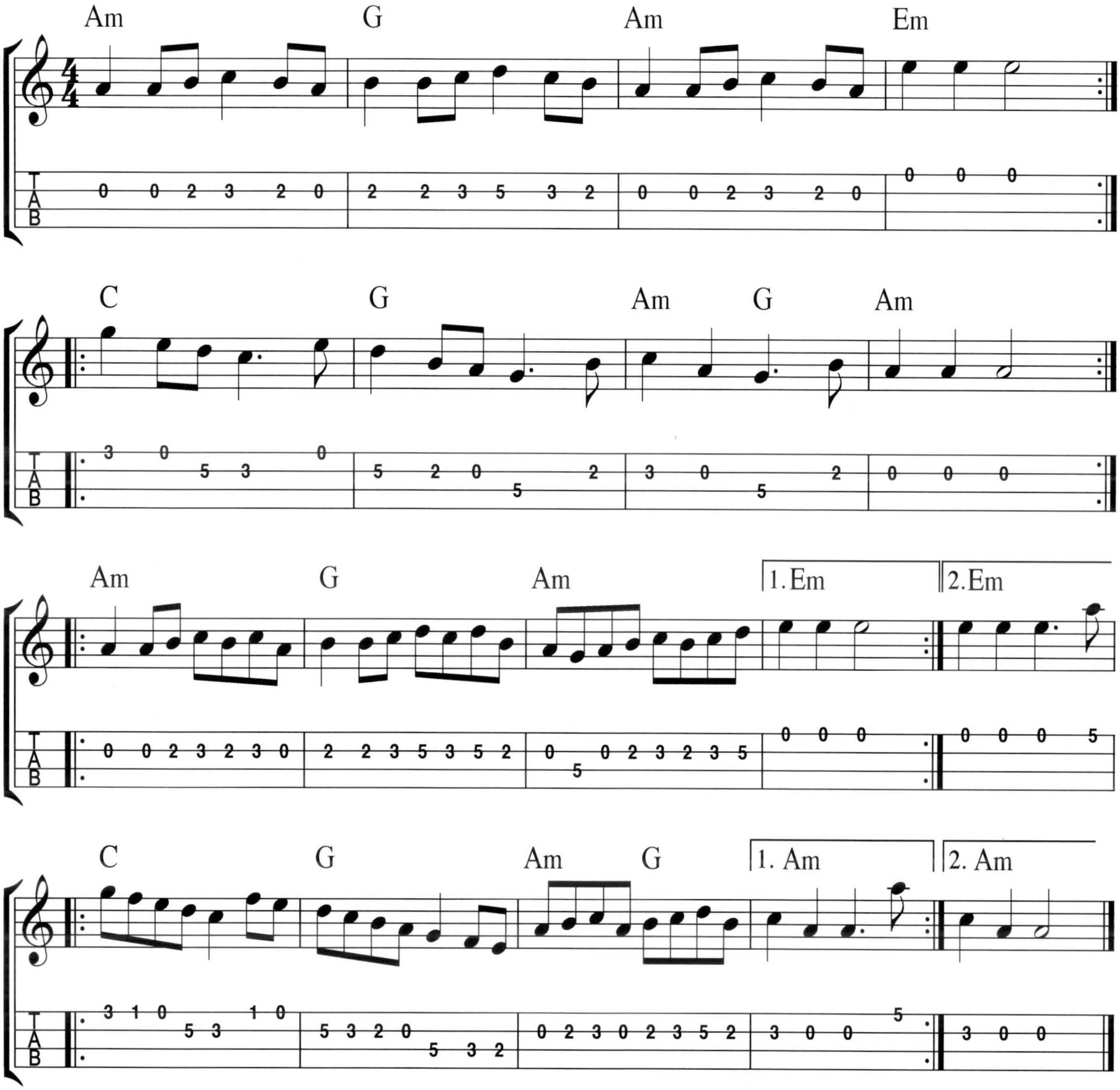
Am G Am Em
C G Am G Am
Am G Am 1.Em 2.Em
C G Am G 1. Am 2. Am

Greensleeves and Pudding Pies

Greenwich Park

The Grenadiers' March

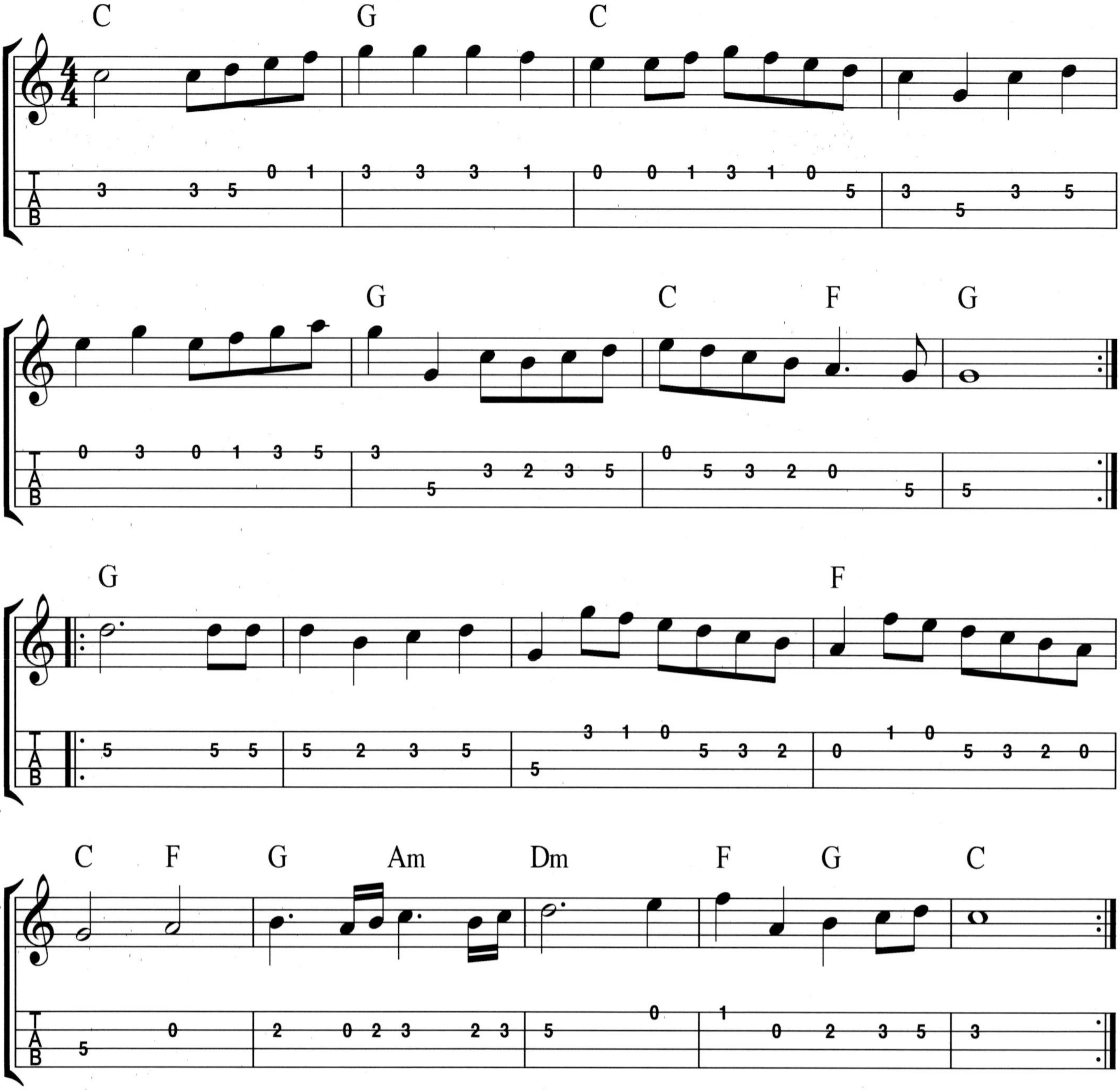

Haphazard

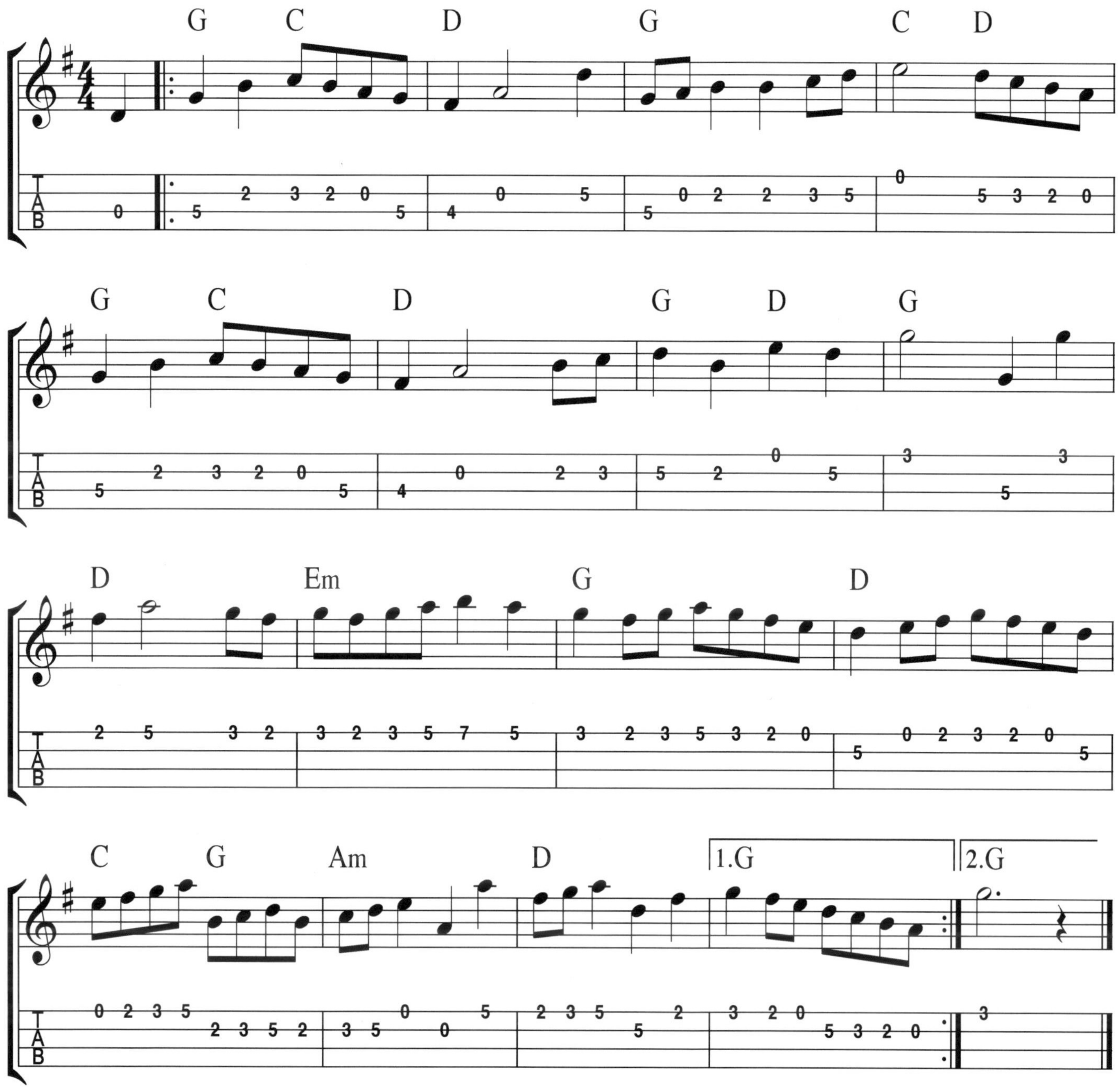
G C D G C D
G C D G D G
D Em G D
C G Am D 1.G 2.G

The Happy Marriage

Hayn's Jig

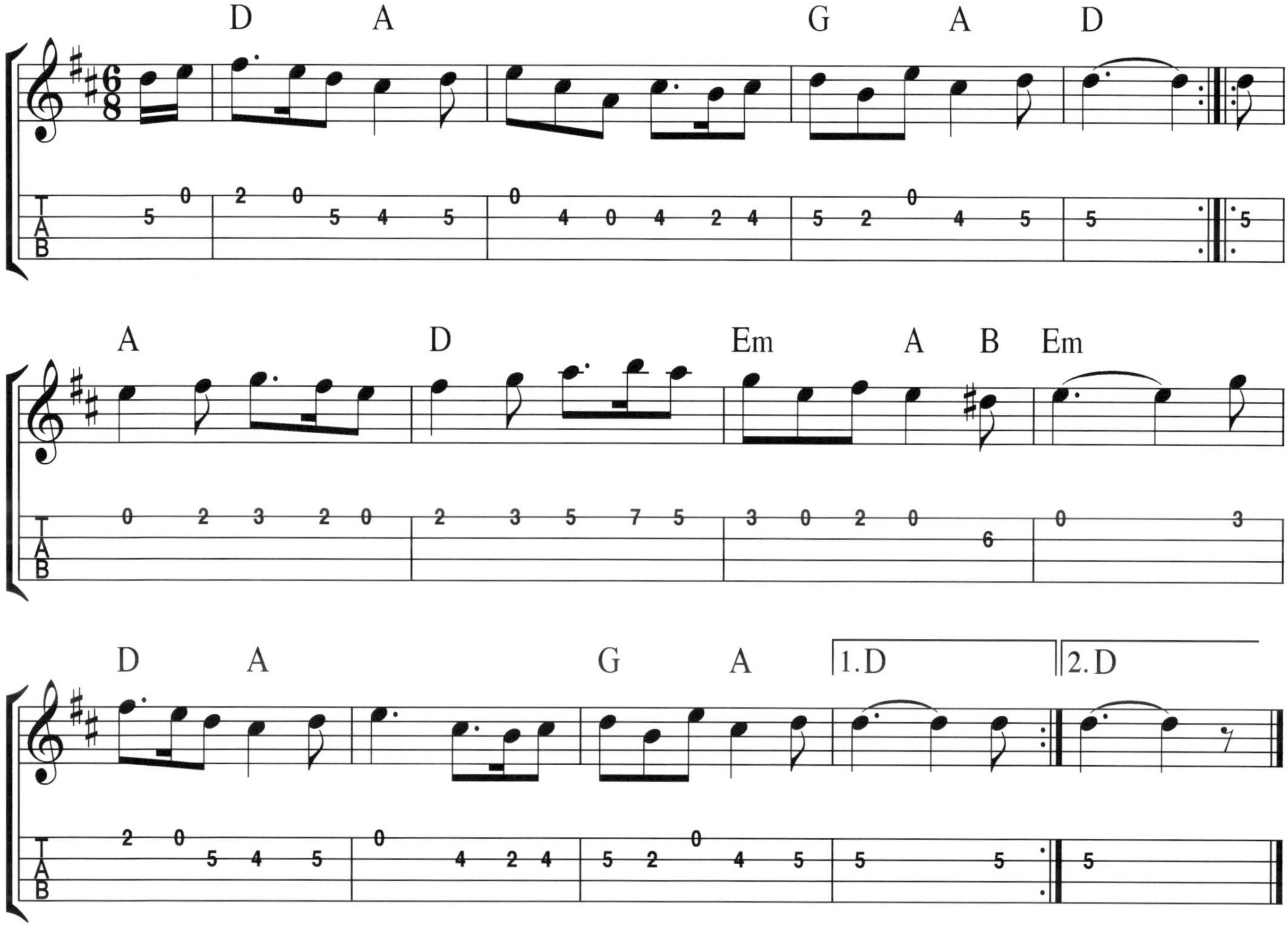
D
A
G
A
D
A
D
Em
A
B
Em
D
A
G
A
1.D
2.D

Heart's Ease

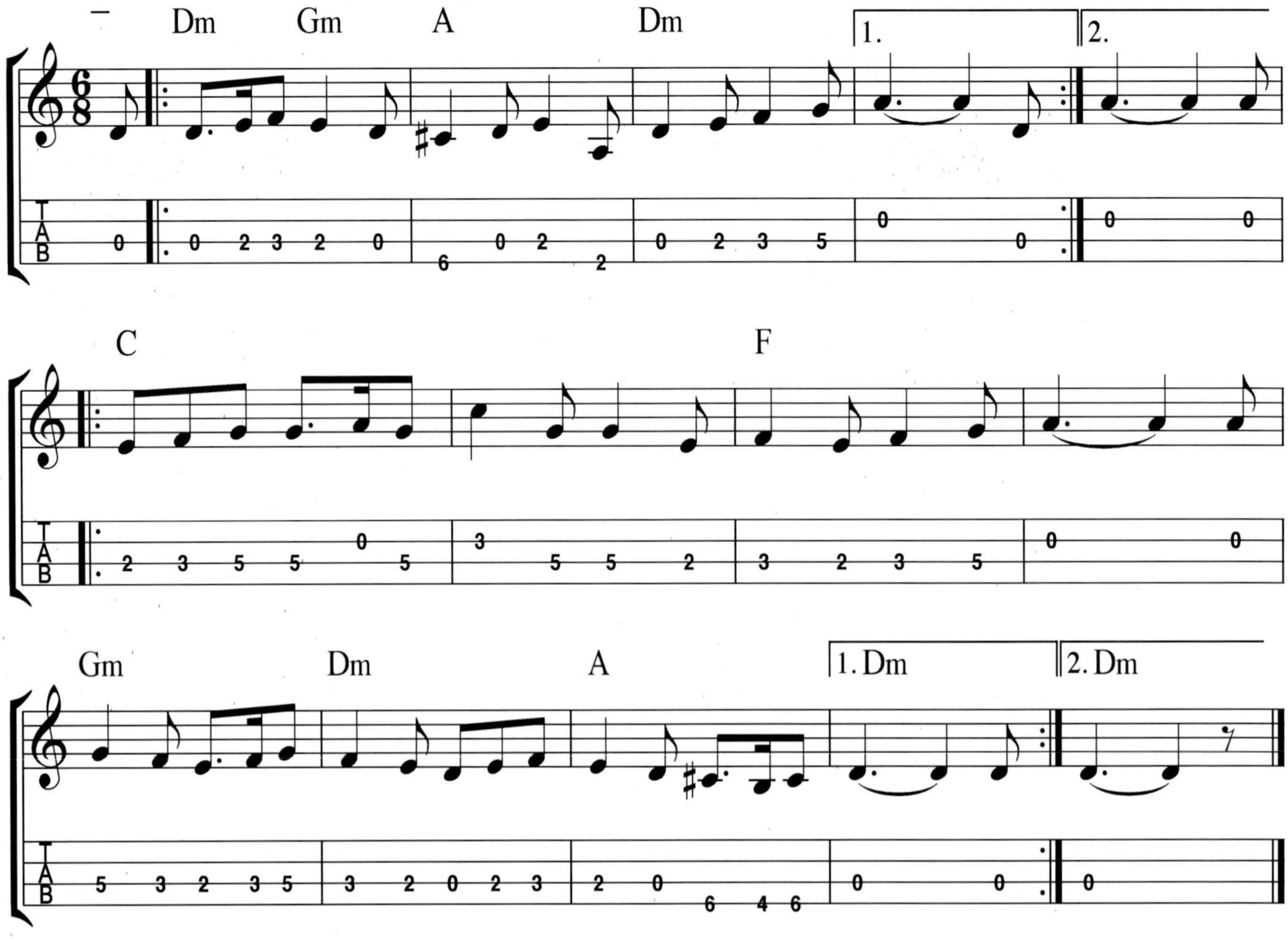
Dm Gm A Dm
1.
2.
C F
Gm Dm A
1. Dm
2. Dm

Hyde Park

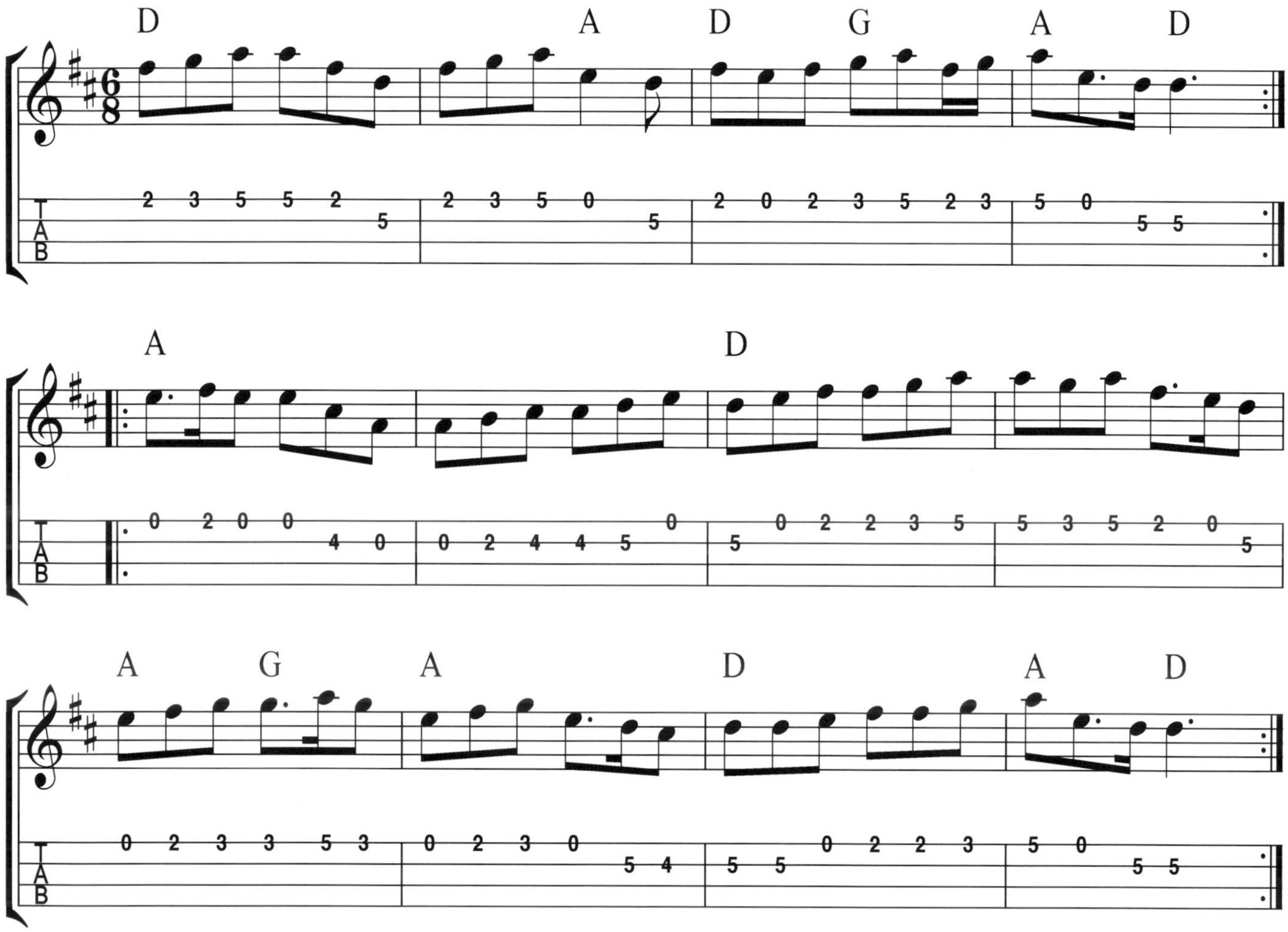
D A D G A D
A D
A G A D A D

An Italian Rant

Jack's Farewell

Jack's Maggot

Jamaica

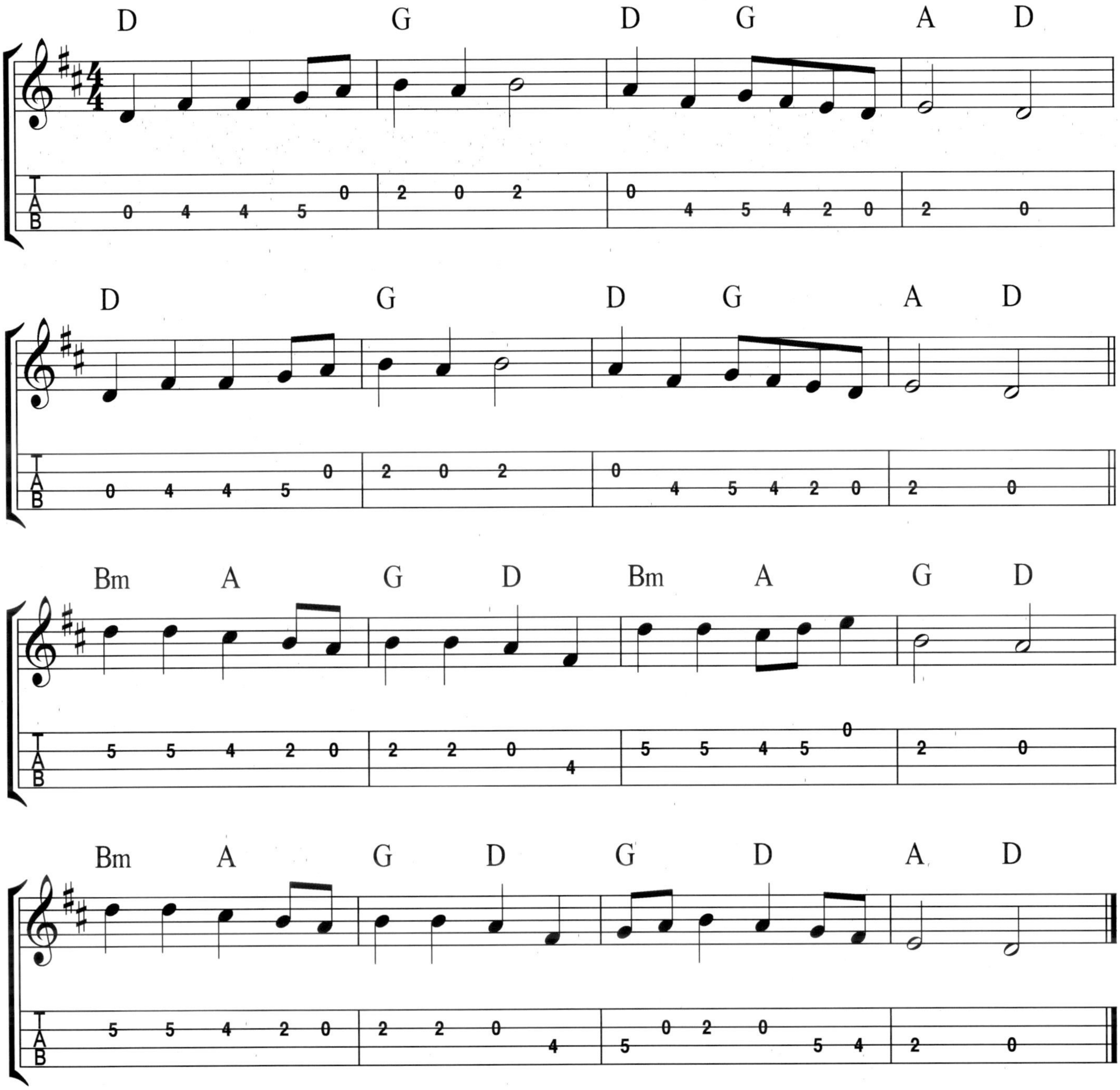
D G D G A D
D G D G A D
Bm A G D Bm A G D
Bm A G D G D A D

The Ladies' Maggot

Ladies of London

Lady Day

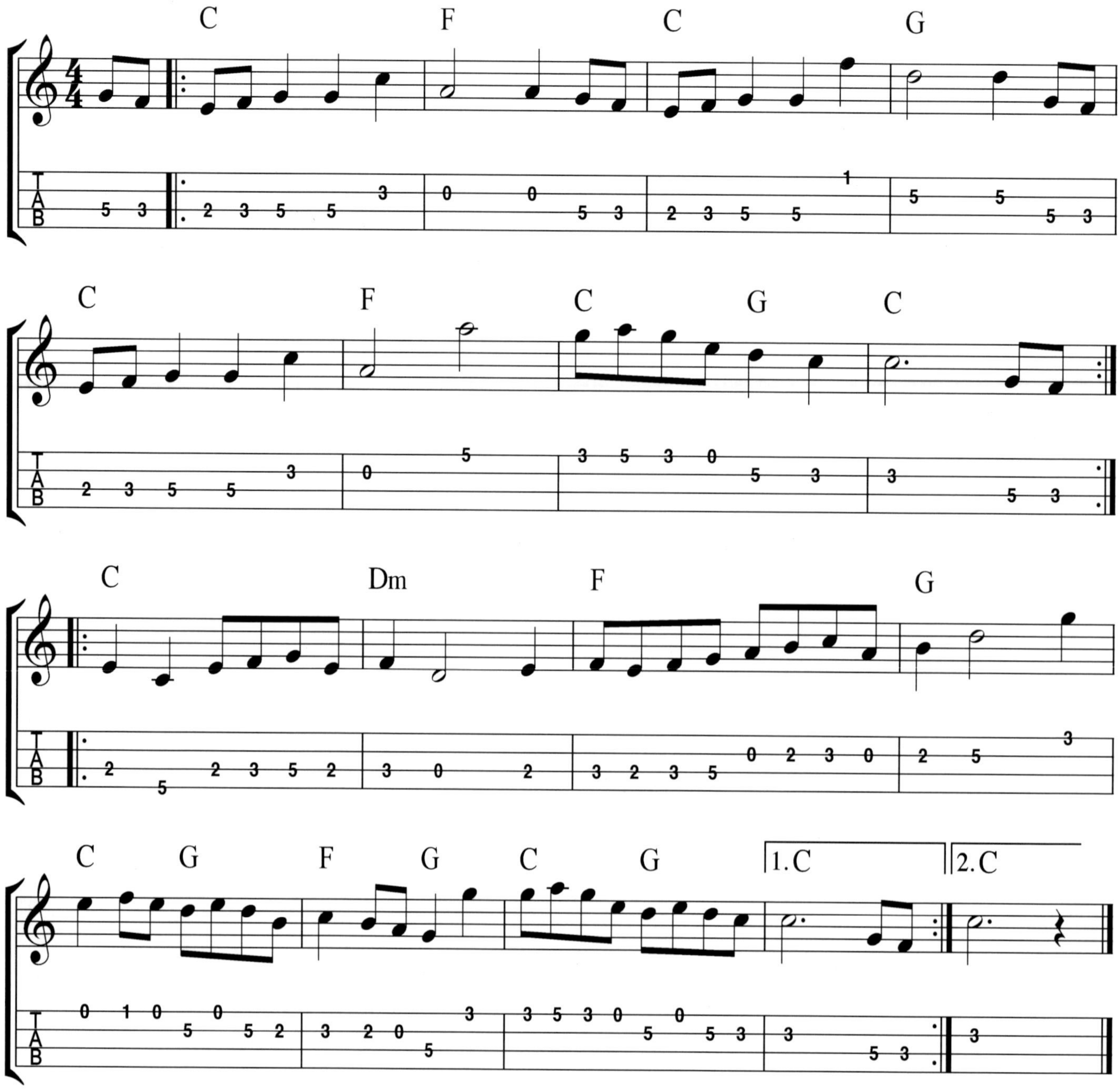
C F C G
C F C G C
C Dm F G
C G F G C G 1.C 2.C

Lady Frances Nevill's Delight

The Last New Vagaries

Lilli Burlero

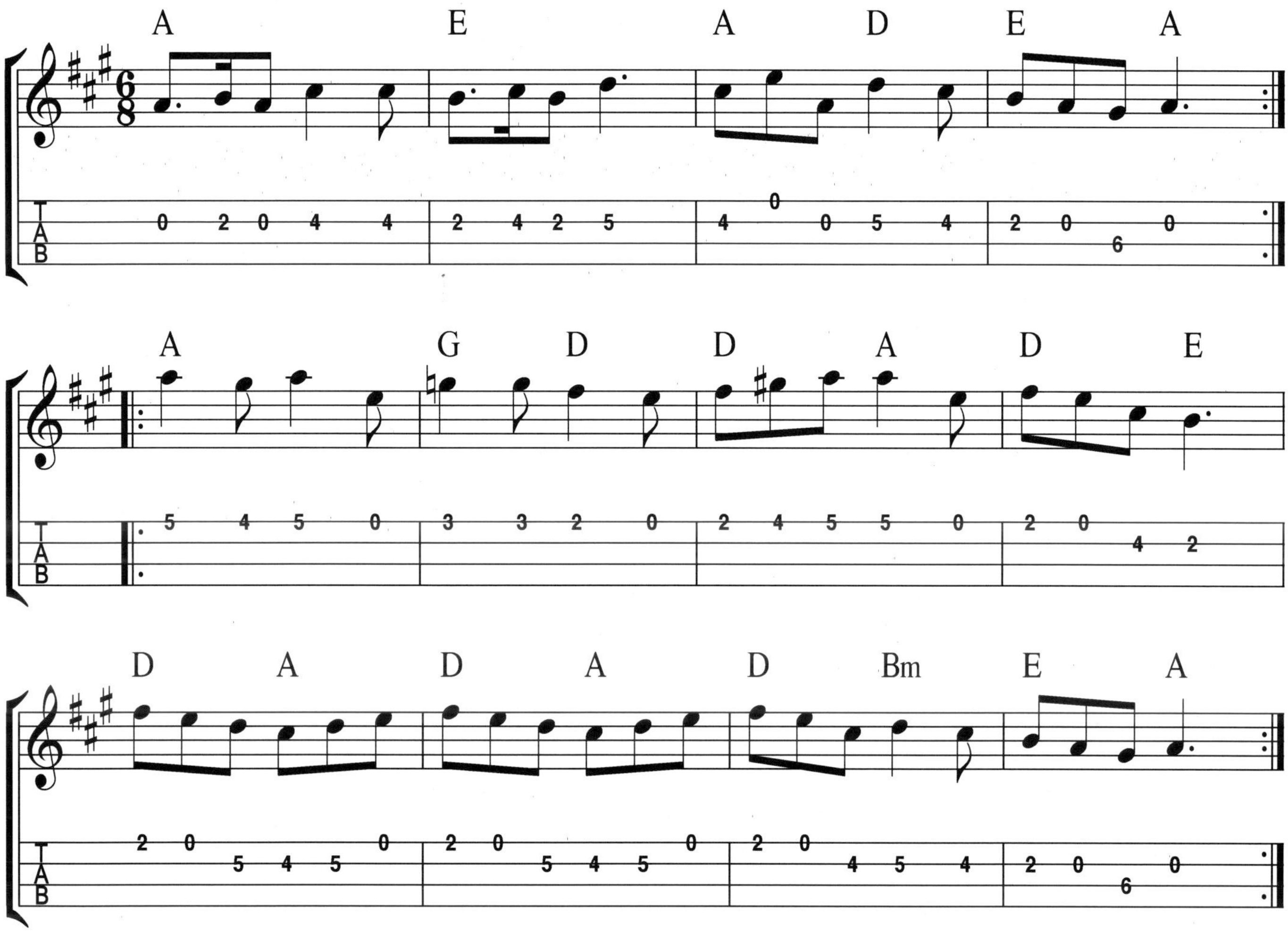

Lord Phoppington

Lull Me Beyond Thee

Mad Dick

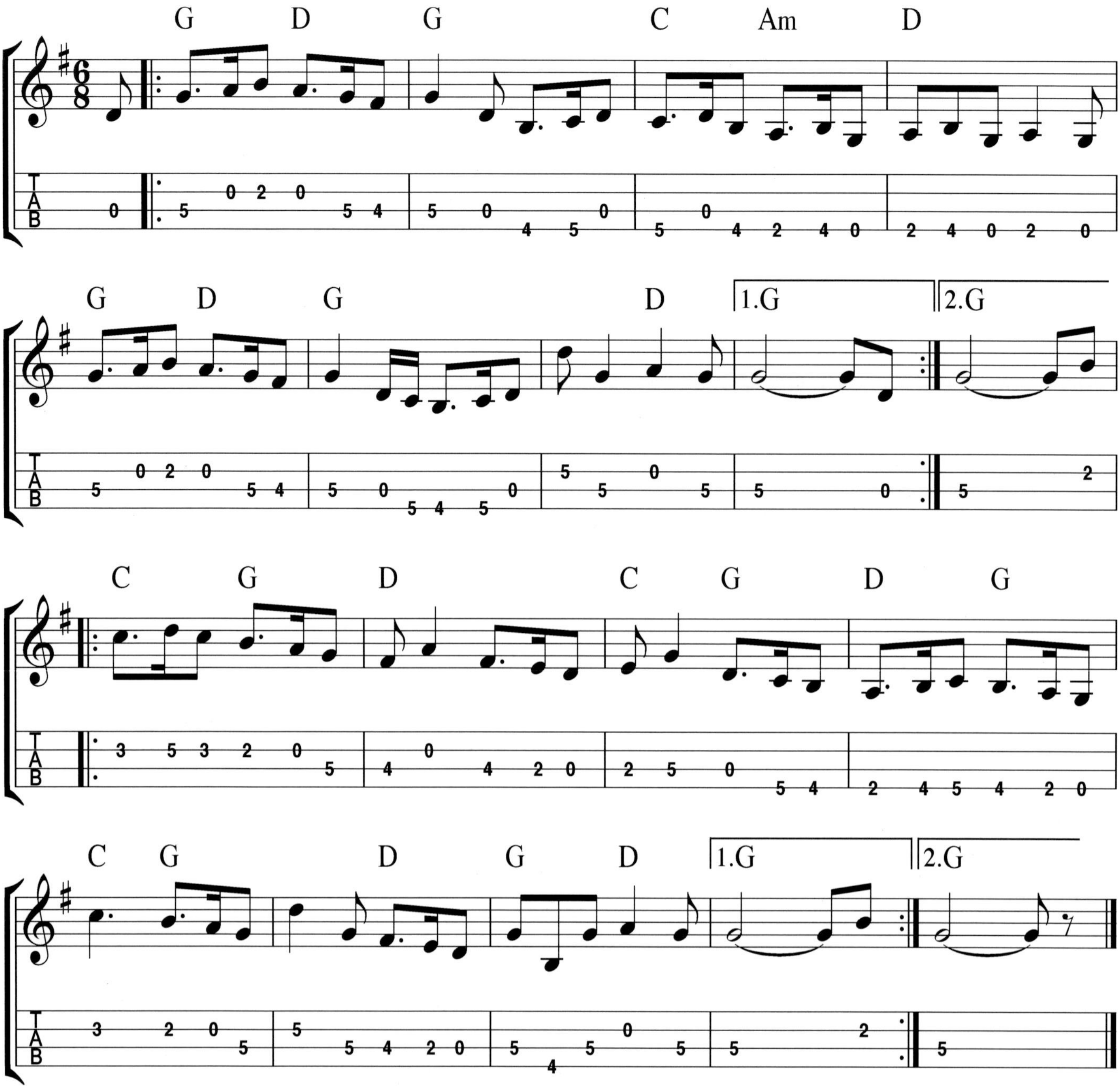
G D G C Am D
G D G D 1.G 2.G
C G D C G D G
C G D G D 1.G 2.G

Maiden Lane

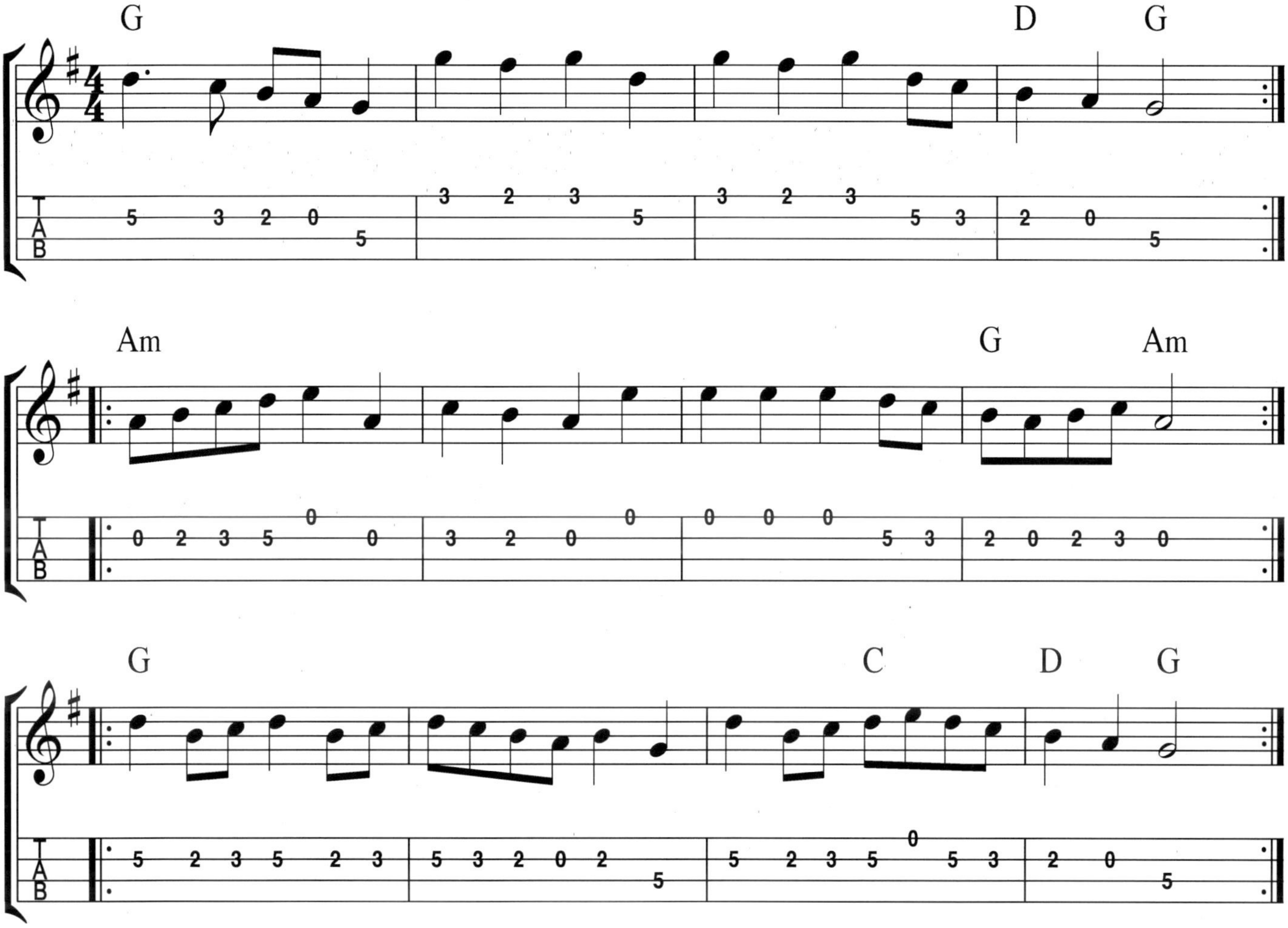

Maid's Morris

Mardike

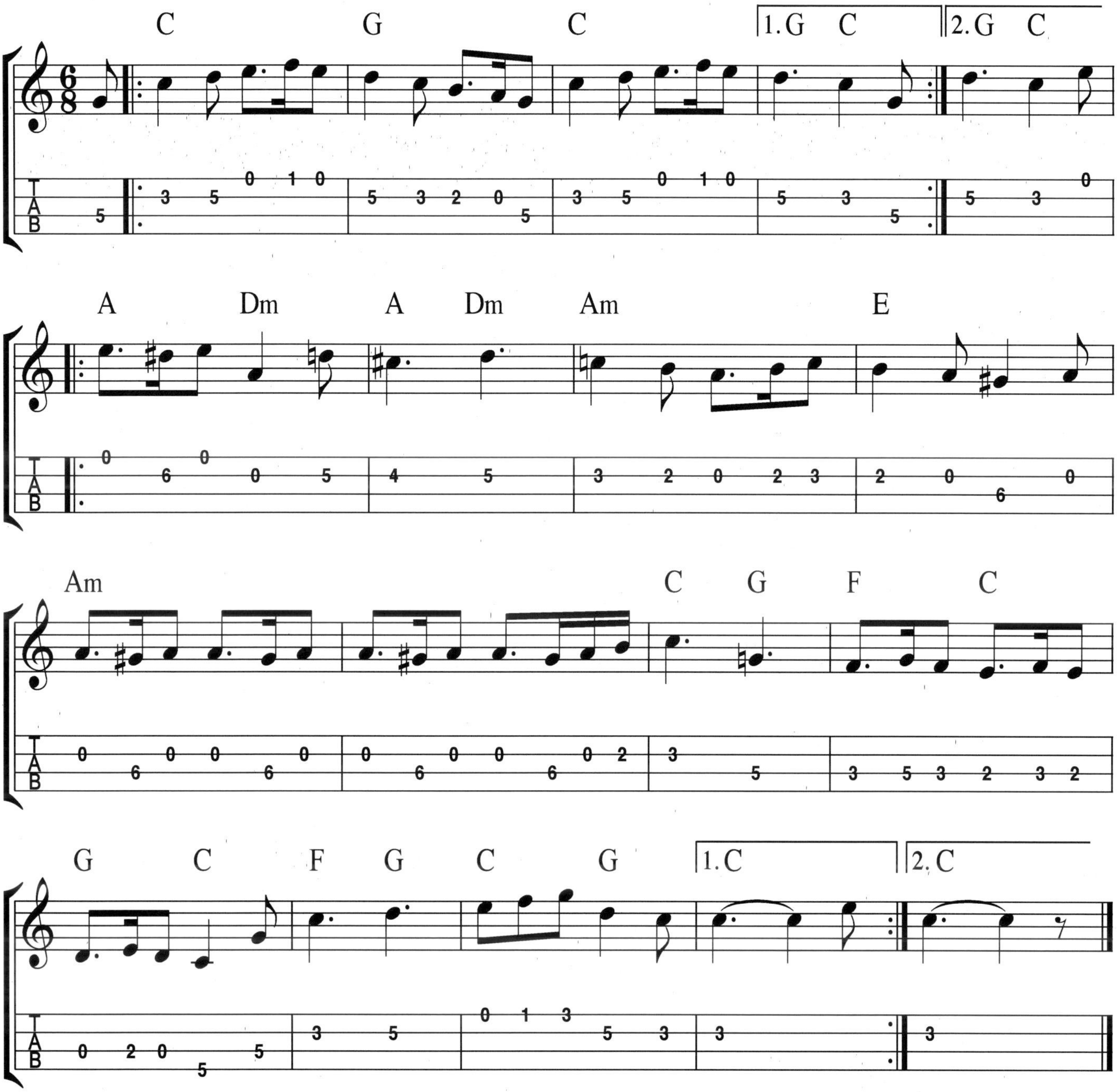
C G C 1.G C 2.G C
A Dm A Dm Am E
Am C G F C
G C F G C G 1.C 2.C

The More the Merrier

Moulson's Jig

Mount Hills

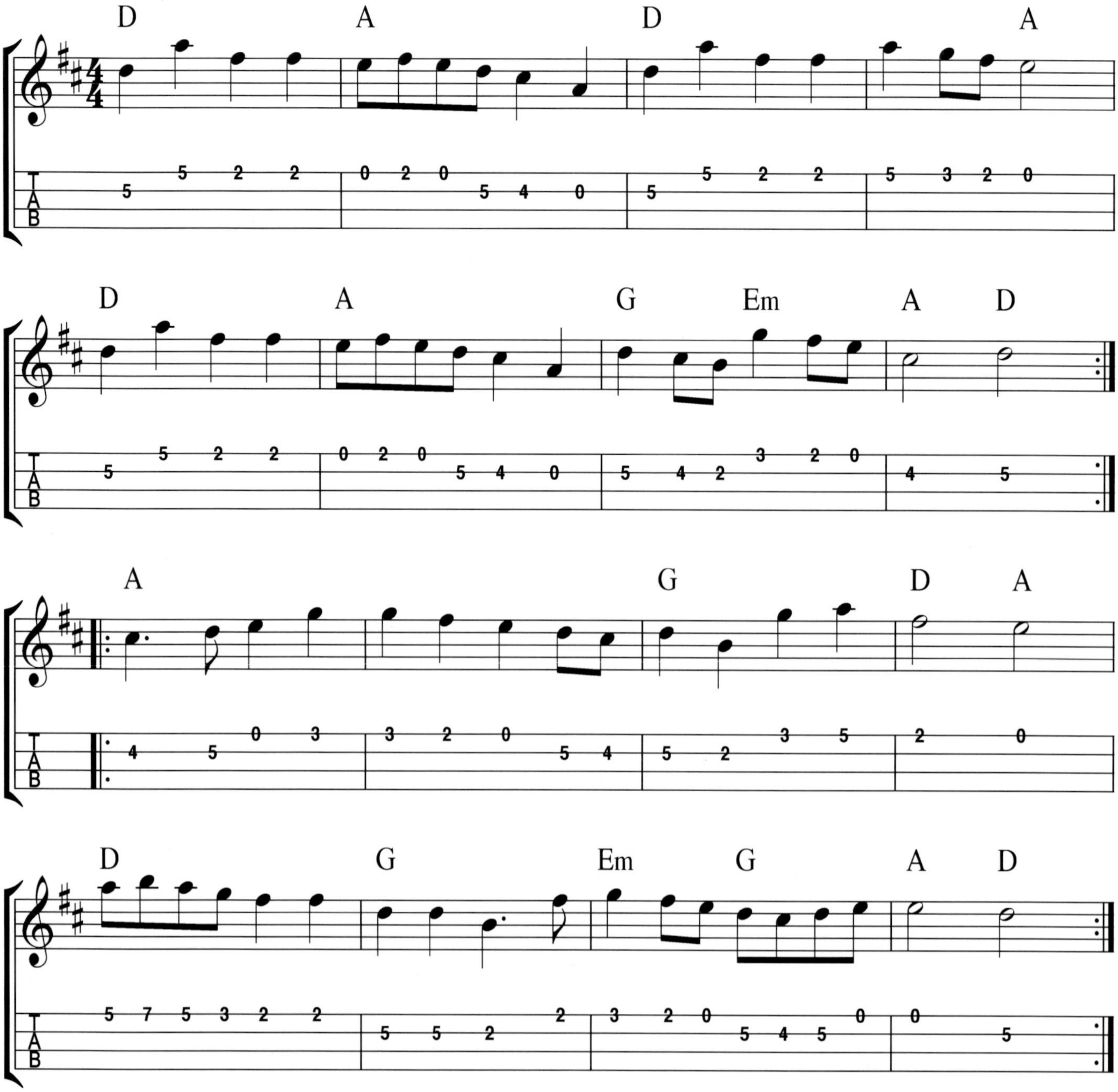
D A D A
D A G Em A D
A G D A
D G Em G A D

Mr. Lane's Maggot

The Mug-House

Never Love Thee More

The New Bourrée

New Metar

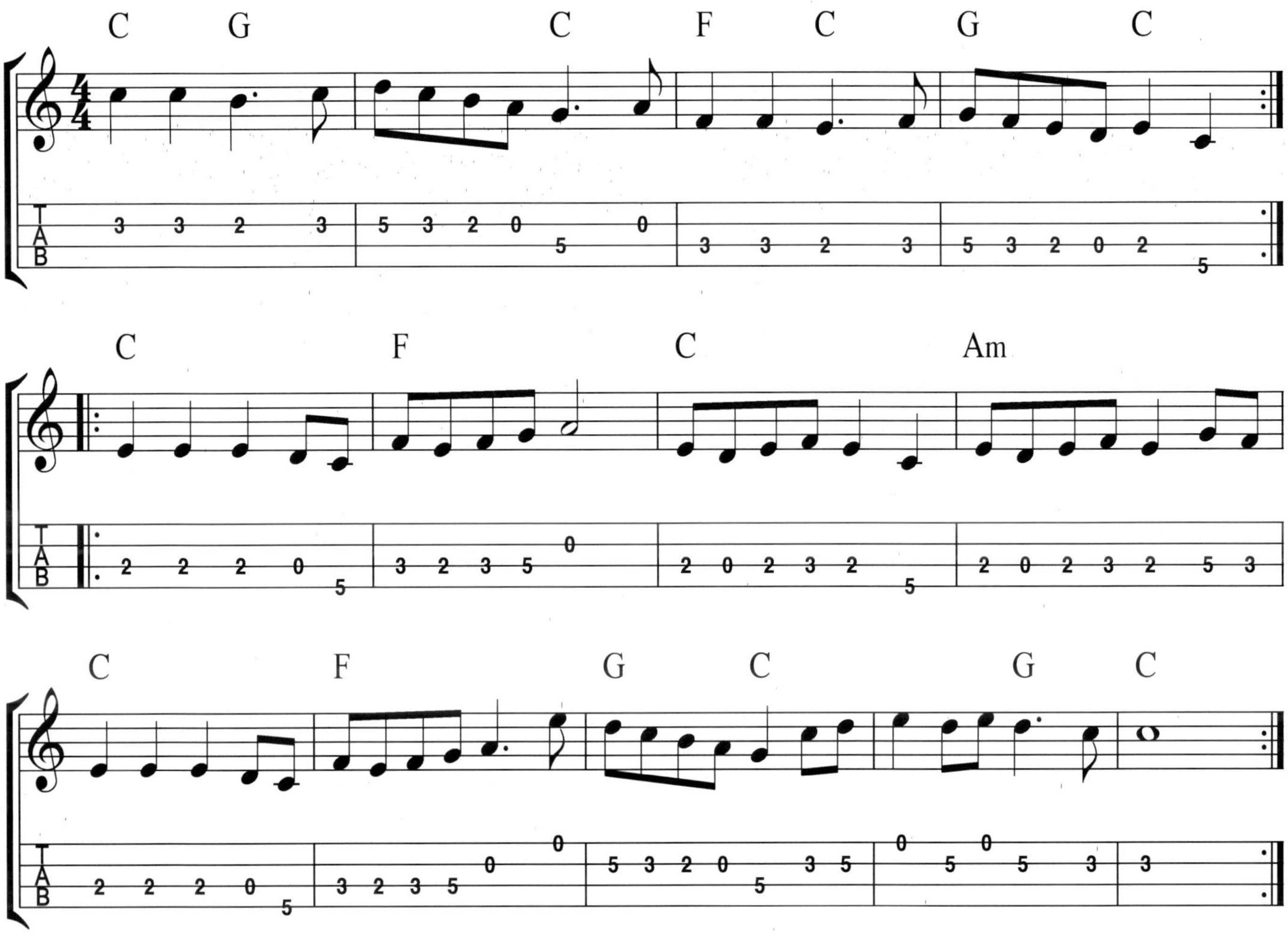
C G C F C G C
C F C Am
C F G C G C

The New New Exchange

A New Rigaudon

Newcastle

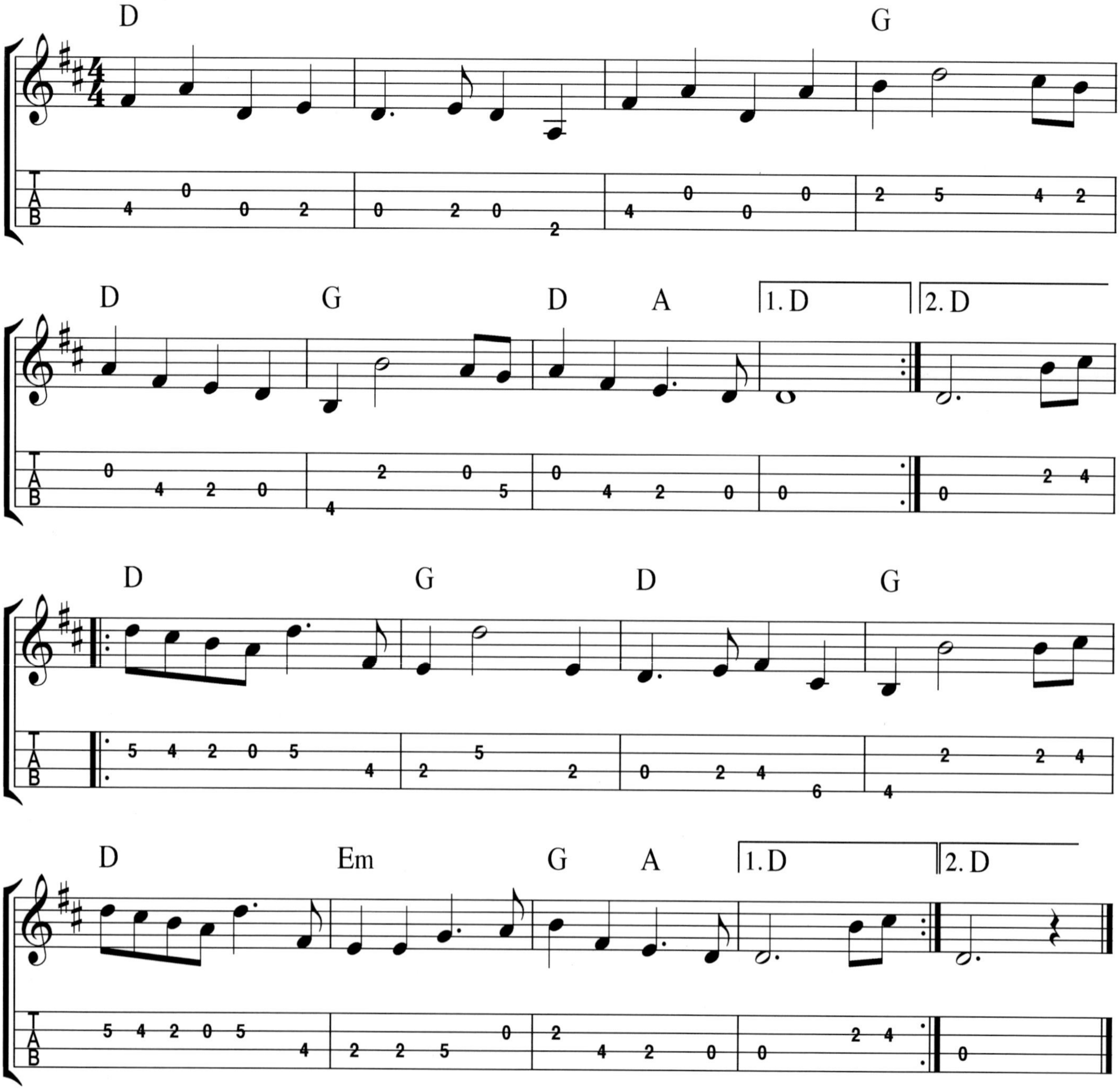
D G
D G D A 1. D 2. D
D G D G
D Em G A 1. D 2. D

Nottingham Castle

Old Noll's Jig

On the Cold Ground

Ormond House

Parson's Farewell

Pell-Mell

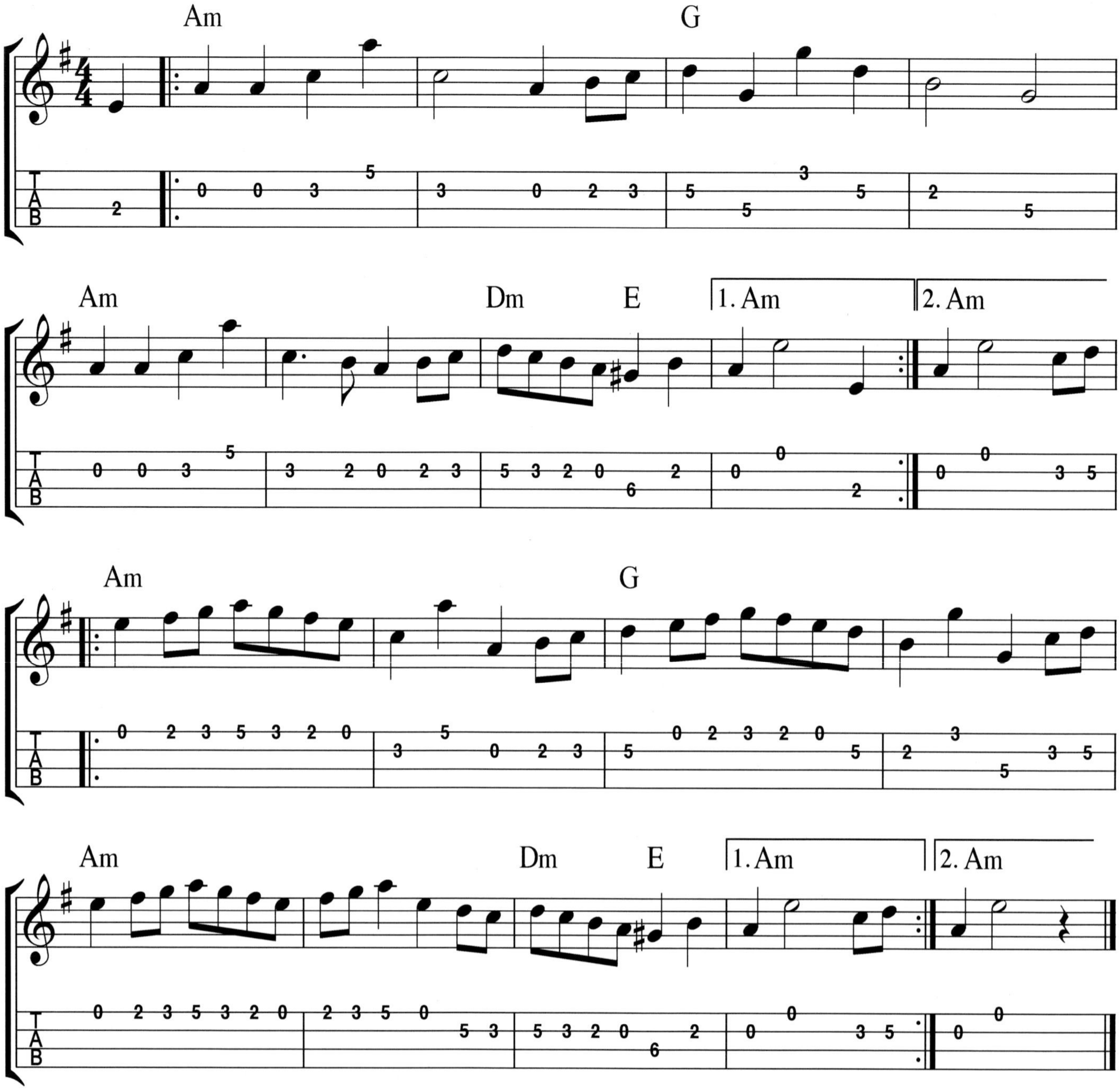
Am
G
Am
Dm
E
1. Am
2. Am
Am
G
Am
Dm
E
1. Am
2. Am

Porter's Dream

Portsmouth

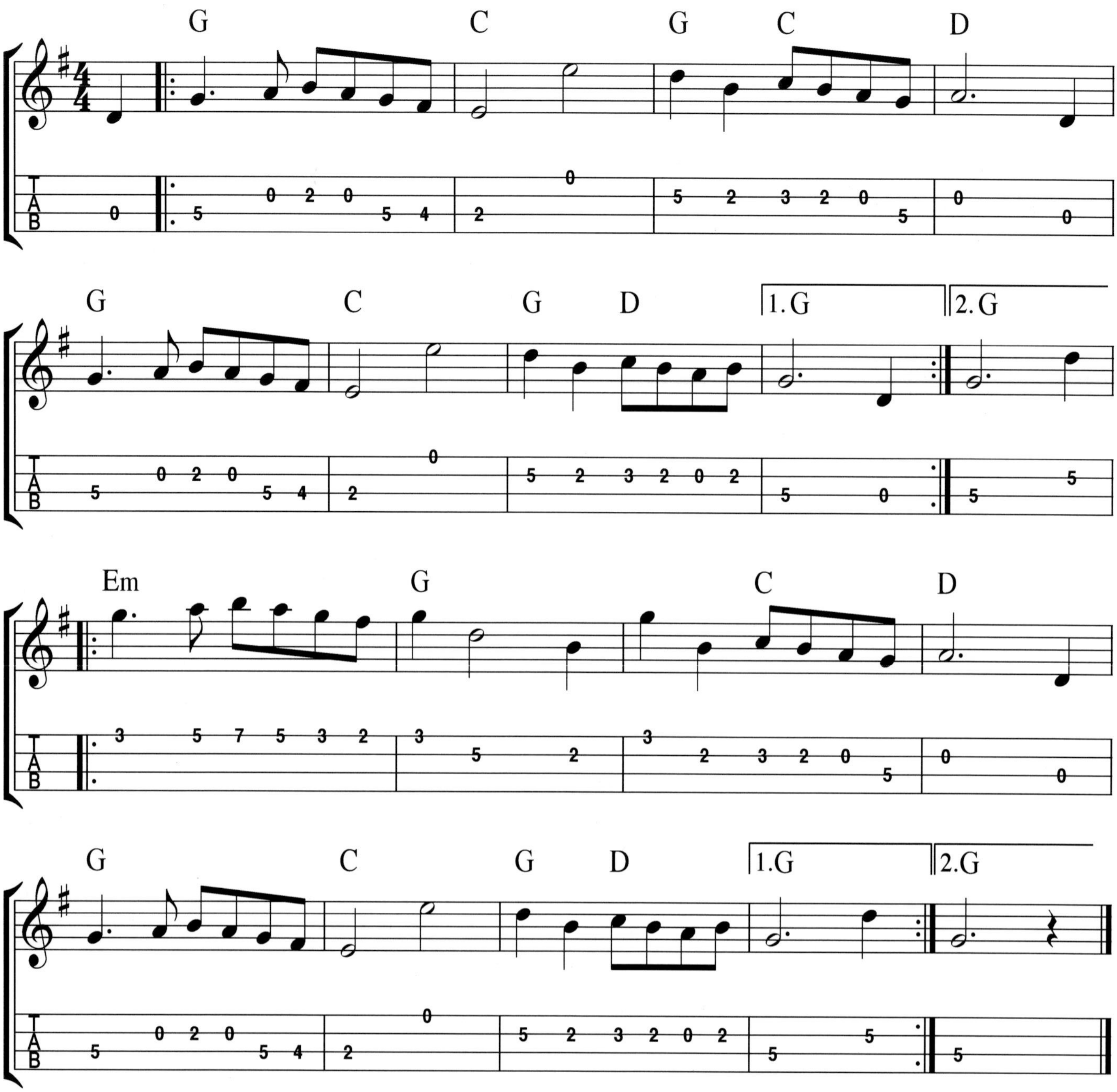
G C G C D
G C G D 1.G 2.G
Em G C D
G C G D 1.G 2.G

Prince George

Prince George's March

Prince Rupert's March

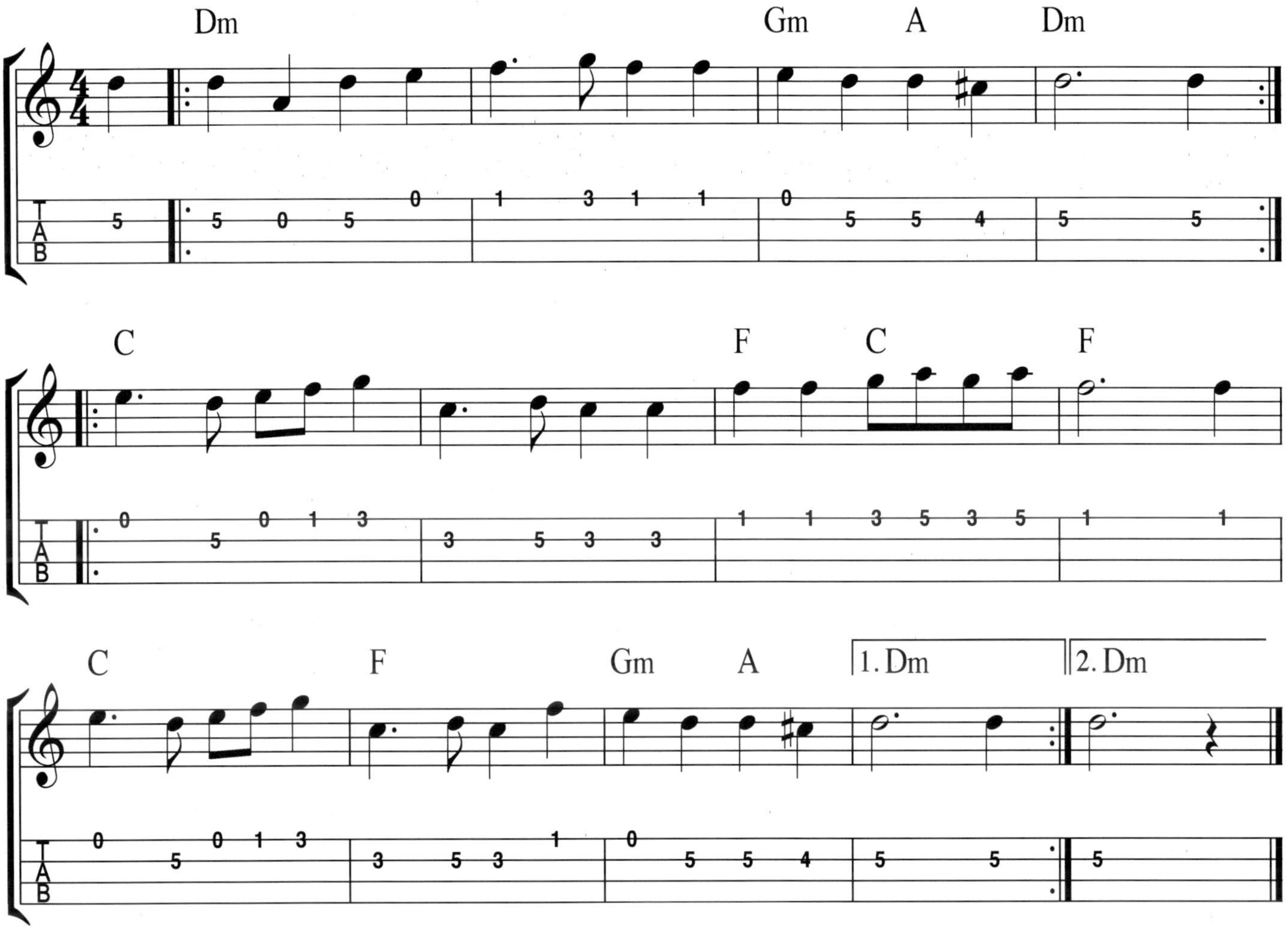

The Princess

Putney Ferry

The Quaker's Grace

The Queen's Birthday

The Rummer

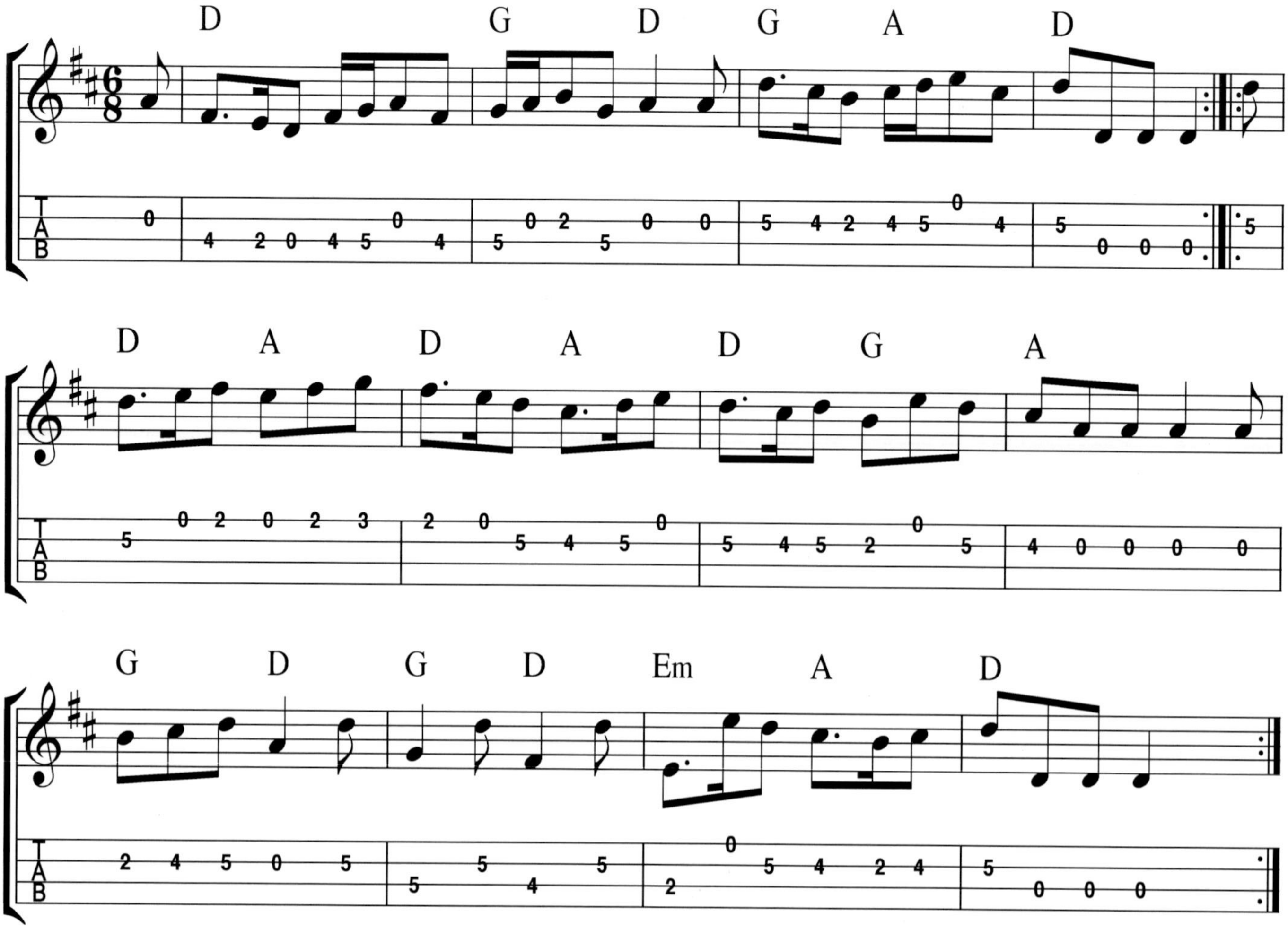
D G D G A D
D A D A D G A
G D G D Em A D

The Shepherd's Daughter

The Siege of Buda

Solomon's Jig

St. Catherine

St. Martins

Am G C C D Em
C G Dm Am Em 1. Am 2. Am
Em Am Em C G C
C F Am Dm Am Em 1. Am 2. Am

St. Martin's Lane

Stanes Morris

Strawberries and Cream

Sweet Kate

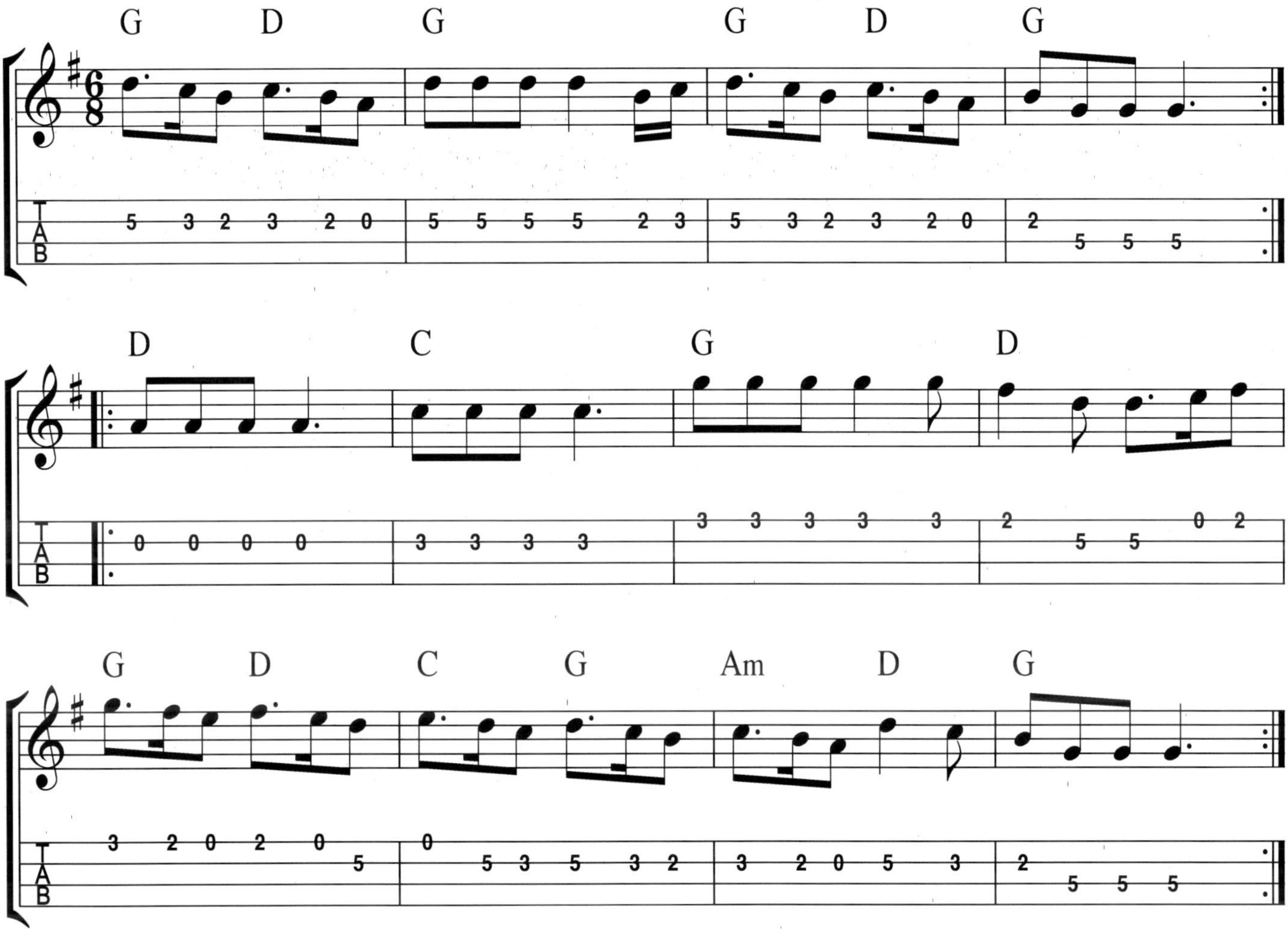
G D G G D G
D C G D
G D C G Am D G

Sweet William

Thomas You Cannot

Twelfth Eve

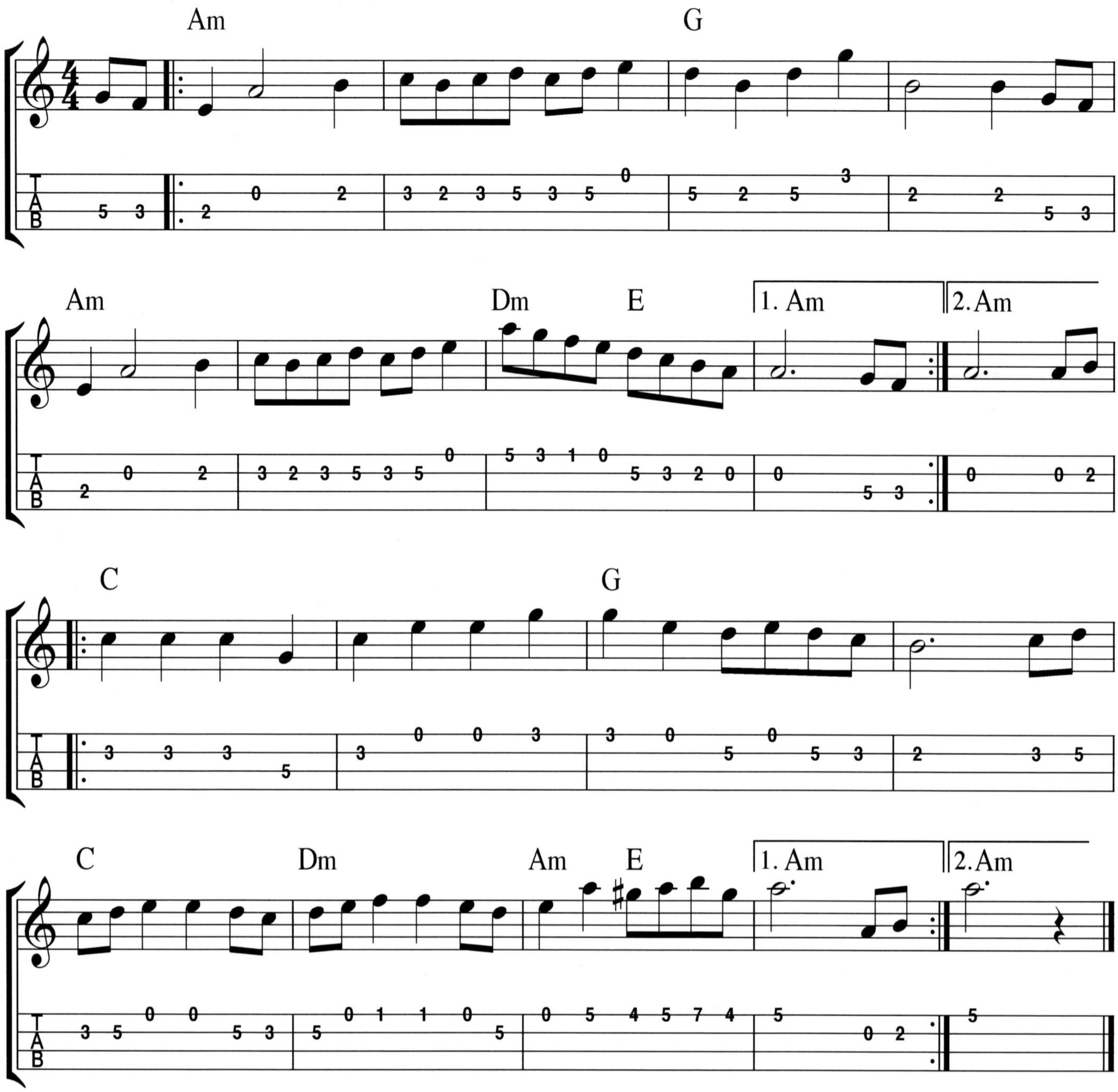
Am G
Am Dm E 1. Am 2.Am
C G
C Dm Am E 1. Am 2.Am

Tythe Pig

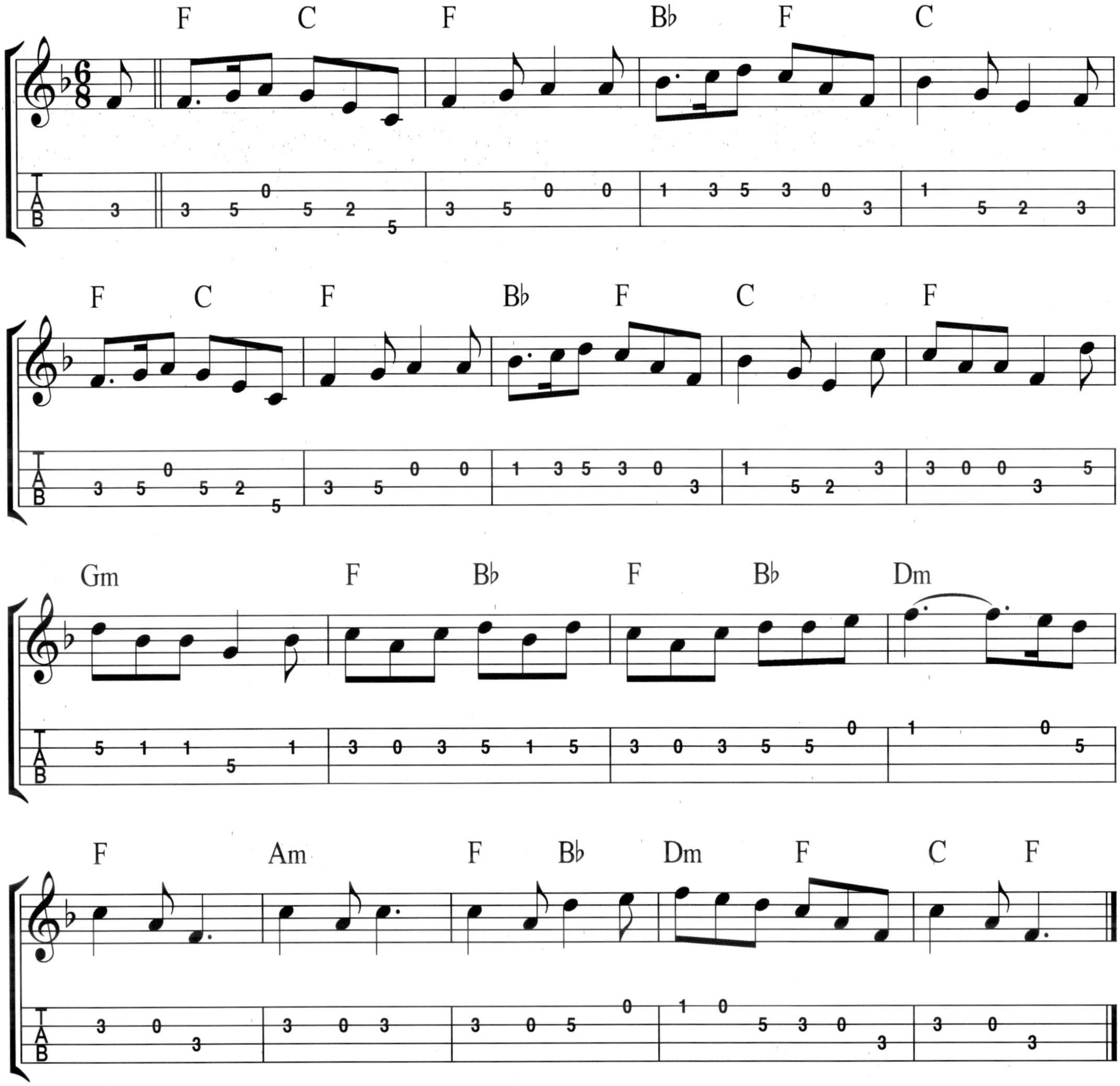
F C F B♭ F C
F C F B♭ F C F
Gm F B♭ F B♭ Dm
F Am F B♭ Dm F C F

Under and Over

Wallingford House

Waltham Abbey

Well Hall

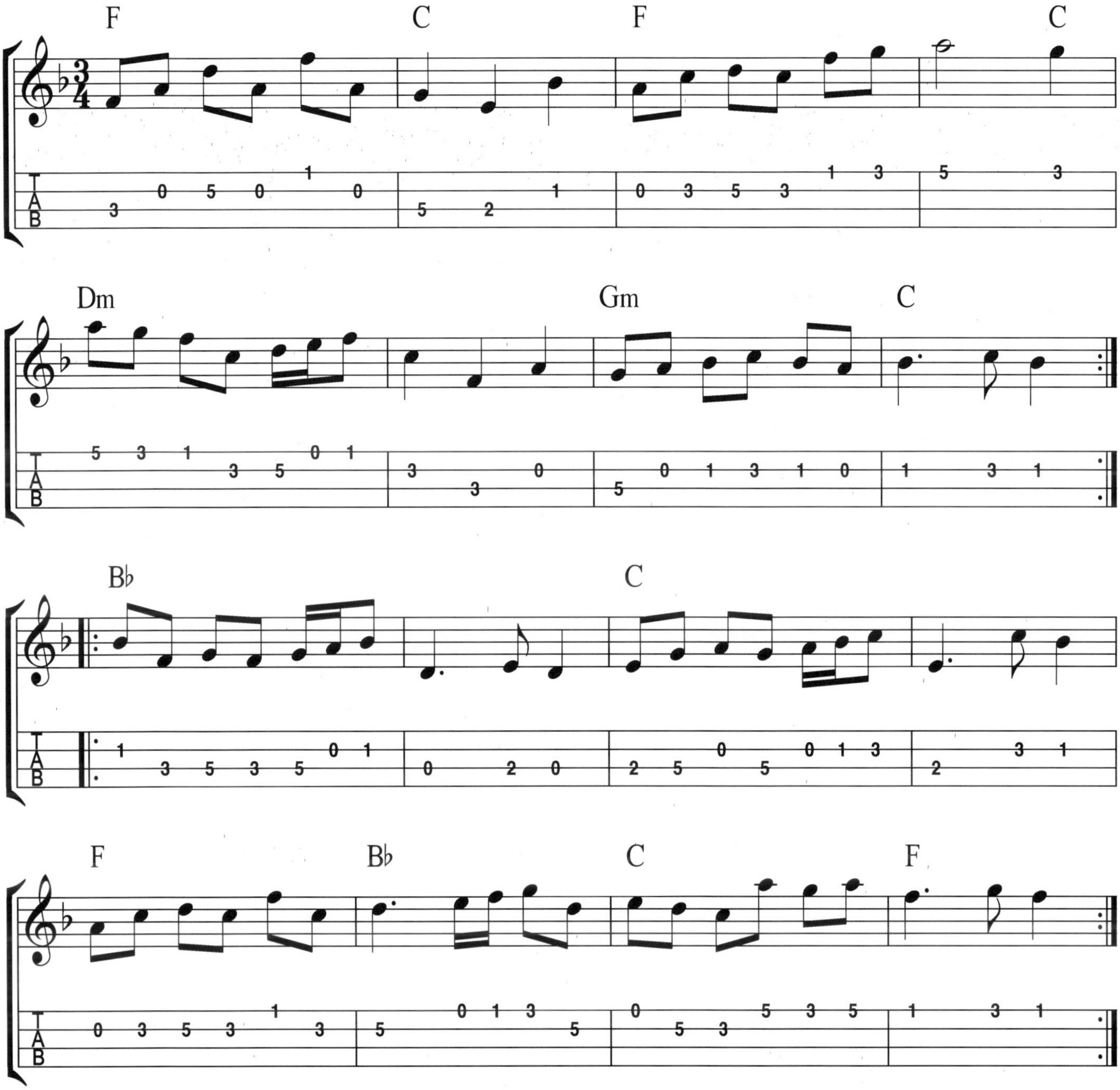
F C F C
Dm Gm C
B♭ C
F B♭ C F

Westmorland

Whitehall Minuet

Wimbleton House

Wooden Shoes

WWW.MELBAY.COM